Karl August Horst

THE QUEST OF
20TH CENTURY GERMAN LITERATURE

With 68 halftones and many line illustrations

Frederick Ungar Publishing Co., New York

*Translated from the German
by Elizabeth Thompson*

First American edition 1971
by arrangement with Nymphenburger Verlagshandlung, Munich

© 1964 by Nymphenburger Verlagshandlung GmbH.
under the title *Anatomy and Trends
of 20th Century German Literature*

Printed in Germany
Library of Congress Catalog Card Number 71-165017
ISBN 0-8044-0402-0

Contents

List of halftone illustrations

Whence and whither?

The story of the German who on his first visit to Italy astonished the local inhabitants by asking the way from the station to his hotel in the lofty language of Dante could probably no longer happen to-day. However, I have been told on good authority that during the last war a German soldier who had studied the Romance languages at college once preached the Sunday sermon in a village in the south of France and revealed a better knowledge of *provençal* than was boasted by most people in the district. There is something comforting about the anecdote: it shows us that the shortest and most direct way to understand the culture of a foreign country is through the language, a fact which is often forgotten in our confused discussions about problems of political constitution, social institutions and economic interests. Whatever the meaning we attribute to the word 'culture', it will always be based on the knowledge that something is entrusted to our care and protection; something which we must go on developing to the best of our ability. There is a tendency in relatively stable times to regard culture as a kind of property. We are proud of the wealth of paintings, sculpture and other works of art which fills our museums; we list the fine buildings which distinguish a town and point them out to strangers as interesting sights, or, mentioning the repertory of the various theatres, we ask our foreign guest: "Would you rather see a classical play or a modern one?"

Culture which is exhibited in this manner, or offered for choice, in the end appears like a house in which so much furniture has accumulated in the course of the centuries that the last pieces to arrive are relegated to the humblest positions. Does not a time come when this mass of furniture should be drastically reduced, leaving only the vital essentials? This feeling that history and culture were something oppressive, leaving no air for the present to breathe, was beginning to appear in Germany towards the end of the last century. Those who of

Culture is something in which we share, not something to be possessed

5

Cultural development
inevitably brings with it a time
to forget, as well as the time
to remember

their own free will, or under compulsion, leave the edifice of culture, however, see it in an entirely different light. They come to realize that culture is never a clearly defined, permanent entity, but rather in constant process of development, always undergoing change and not even sure of its claim to be at home on the soil of its native country. How often have great minds had to go into exile! The Roman poet Ovid tuned his Latin tongue to more plaintive tones on the shores of the Black Sea. The philosopher Seneca, who spent long years of exile on the wild and rocky island of Corsica, observed what ample space the humblest cabin offers when inhabited by the virtues of the mind. He also reminded us that the distance to the stars is the same from any place on earth. From this we see that culture is not simply property but a spiritual possession the value of which is judged by whether it can compensate for the sorrow of separation from all familiar things, for exposure to distress and menace, and prove its worth as a source of fortitude.

European culture is not mainly
concerned with preserving
traditional values but rather
with creating new ones

Seeking a comparison with which to illustrate the two aspects of the enigmatic phenomenon of culture with all the force of a legend, I find most suitable the story of interminable travels and exile told by Homer in the Odyssey. What reason should we have to talk of Ulysses if there had been no Trojan War, no quarrel among the gods and no wanderings and long-delayed return? We know that Ulysses did not lightly abandon his native land, the little island of Ithaca. There he was guarded by his ancestors, by the spirits of the trees, the water and the soil, who in the course of many generations had concluded a pact with men, maintained by piety in return for protection. Out at sea, on the other hand, the individual was relentlessly exposed to conflicting powers. Fortune was capricious and inscrutable, wrapping him in a cloud which obscured his view yet did not protect him from the jealousy of another god who, finding a propitious moment, could send him to his doom.

This story, while teaching us something about the progress of culture, or the civilization of the mind, also illustrates how periods of domestic security accompanied by gradual development alternate with periods of bold adventure and sudden changes of fortune. As we generally think in opposites and call attitudes which do not conform to our idea of life historical, we tend when considering the notion of culture to stress the particular aspect which appears to us at the moment to constitute its essential nature. Ulysses building himself a raft on the shore of Ogygia is not the same as the Ulysses who drove his oxen over the fields in Ithaca. In times of necessity culture develops an inventive trait and reverts to an artisanal and experimental character. It no longer remains within its habitual, domestic sphere, pursuing its development there, but launches out into unwonted practices, seeking for suitable means to overcome a problem or to achieve an ardently desired goal.

The Odyssey of culture is reflected in the history of literature, and its two different aspects must always be considered: the domestic and settled on the one hand, and on the other the adventurous and agitated; the culture securely possessed or believed to be so and the cultural development being sought. Ithaca — point of departure as well as final destination of the journey, which the returned traveller, shipwrecked and only recognized by his dog, reconquers by the strength of his own arm, and the storm-tossed incertitude of the ocean, with terrors and outrage on many shores and then the descent into the underworld where, fed on the blood of the sacrifice, the dead return to life again.

It need hardly be said which state of culture was reflected in German literature in the first half of this century. The situation in most European countries was the same, although the new spirit which was breaking through revealed itself in different forms depending on the tenets it was renouncing and the habits it was breaking with. The culture of France has an Ithaca which is not the same as the native land of German culture. The adventure of Spanish literature will always start from a certain unnamed spot in the Mancha and be heroic yet frugal as was Don Quixote, while that of the English will eternally revolve around the fabulous island of Shakespeare's *Tempest* or the realm of Spenser's *Faery Queen*.

In discussing a period of literary history for which we can only give provisional dates, since we start from the departure of literature for an unknown goal and cannot foresee the final outcome because we are still too deeply involved in the hazards of the journey, it is advisable to consider the latter in the light of whence it started and what distinctive form or feature it rejected, rather than to profess knowledge of a final goal of which no-one knows whether it will ever be reached or if it may not even turn out to be as illusory as a mirage. With regard to the fate of Ulysses, too, we know that opinions differ. Homer tells us

The cultural situation at the turn of the century

that he returned to Ithaca, defeated the pretentious suitors and was again master in his own house, in the full dignity and enjoyment of the conjugal love which the faithful Penelope had never betrayed. Dante tells a different story: of a Ulysses who never came home, whose adventures carried him ever onward — towards a distant pole, a magnetic mountain which dragged his ship out of its homeward orbit. Comparing the two versions, it is hard to decide which ending we should prophesy for the Odyssey of literature. Will it return to human habit in a world which lives in harmony with the soul or will it reach out beyond the horizon of the inhabited earth towards the pole where the laws and fatality governing its eternal wanderings shall be revealed? Gravity draws a stone back to earth when it has passed the vertex of its trajectory. However, we know that there are realms in which gravity no longer prevails. We know there are realms in which everything is different.

The conviction that 'everything could also be quite different' lies at the origin of the adventurous journey on which literature embarked in the first half of this century. Without gravitation a parabola becomes a spiral which either moves away from its centre along a path of ever widening radius or plunges towards it in ever diminishing coils. The boundlessness of unlimited distance from its own point of departure and the plunge into self-annihilation are the Scylla and Charybdis between which the human mind must navigate to-day.

Experience with time

The simplest way of imparting information about the literature of a certain period is to follow the method of an exhibition or museum catalogue. Lyric verse is presented in the first room, narrative poetry in the second, drama in the third, only the most important works being selected for inclusion. The exhibits may be arranged in different order and classified according to different aspects, for instance the trends of thought or style which appear to predominate in the period in question. There is, however, a serious consideration which prevents us from adopting this course with regard to the literature of the past fifty or sixty years. A personal experience may be used to illustrate this.

Many years ago, in a second-hand book shop, I came across a book which I immediately bought. It was only a year younger than myself and bore the title *Das Grosse Jahr,* and below that the date 1914/15. It was the year-book issued by the leading German literary publisher of the time for the first year of the Great War.

Readers of my generation, unless they are the most hard-boiled aesthetes or the driest of specialists, will immediately want to know what became of the writers who raised their voices at that fateful moment for their country, in the course of the following ten or twenty years. Well-known names figure in the table of contents, names which conjure up the image of that 'other Germany' which opposed the degradation of the nation, voluntarily or under compulsion went into exile and, in so far as its representatives survived, found an utterly changed country after the second world war. Is the expression 'German literature' really appropriate with reference to these patriots who were to go into exile twenty years later? And which Germany do we then mean? At any rate we cannot succeed in separating the literary works of these writers from their personal fate, not only because the memory of the shadow of war and persecution

Contempory German literature does not present a uniform aspect

Emigrants

remains alive in the minds of their contemporaries, but for the incomparably more serious reason that the transformation or complete shattering of the old way of life and its accepted values had already been heralded in their works with something of prophetic anticipation.

Thomas Mann, who as a champion of humanity rendered inestimable services to the name of German literature abroad, clearly recognized that society and genius can seldom be reconciled, that solitude and suffering are the lot of the great, who generally live in conflict with their time. He held Nietzsche in high esteem and adopted his doctrine that the artist and the free man are only bound by their own code of morals. However, he was also fully aware of the discipline necessary in order to maintain the liberty thus acquired at a level worthy of human dignity. Nietzsche's was an aggressive ideal, but it implied mental discipline. It was dictated by the will, but a will which clearly understood its own psychology. This was for Thomas Mann the point of greatest significance in Nietzsche and was the reason why he extolled him on several occasions as "Erkenntnis-Lyriker" — poet of perception. Perception: this implies the conviction that the artist — and particularly the writer — must always keep pace with contemporary learning, but all the knowledge of his age will be of no service to him unless he transforms it into his own, personal truth. When, in the twenties, movements arose which claimed to follow Nietzsche, but in reality only skimmed the metaphysical cream off his doctrine while obscuring his psychological lucidity by vague effusions in support of irrational impulses, Thomas Mann was one of the first to take up a critical stand in opposition, ardently defending the achievements of the nineteenth century, on which Nietzsche's ideas were also based. In spite of his liberal attitude, Mann was intolerant of the general application of ideas which could only be sanctioned by the tragic destiny of exceptional individuals. At the same time, with his artistic sensibility, he was aware of the peril which, more particularly in highly developed civilizations, menaces the mind that allows itself to be overwhelmed by the irrational.

In the almanach mentioned earlier there appears a passage from the famous essay in which Mann assigns to Frederick the Great the position in history which Nietzsche had allotted to his great "Willensmensch" — the Man of Will.

Jacket designed by Wilhelm Schulz, 1903

Die Entstehung des „Doktor Faustus"
Roman eines Romans

Hermann Hesse was one of the few who kept aloof from the storm of national enthusiasm in 1914, for he had very soon realized the danger to the mind of collective psychoses. The almanach mentions a narrative work of his: *Knulp*. This vagabond, a descendant of Eichendorff's romantic *Taugenichts*, is a figure we encounter repeatedly in Hesse's works, in many metamorphoses. He is an outsider who does not fit into conventional society and yet never quite succeeds in breaking away from it entirely; he feels oppressed by its pedantic order but still cannot resist a desire to win its approbation. He opposes the habits and moral conventions of a society that believes itself protected by its well-ordered façade against the shadowy side of life, although a single step beyond the threshold suffices to reveal the fallacy of this self-righteous order. Hesse's scepticism regarding conventional morality was justified by the war. If he himself, who came from a cultured home in the little town of Calw in the Black Forest, had not had such profound faith in the intellectual culture of the nineteenth century, he would not have been so deeply shaken by the crisis which shattered his life in 1916. He had had the courage of his convictions and emigrated to Switzerland at the beginning of the war. There he raised an admonishing voice which few, however, understood, let alone took to heart. The reproach which constantly recurred in his writings was that the mind had so lightly abandoned its pride and independence and from one moment to the next surrendered to force and become enslaved by power. There was therefore something wrong with intellectual life. Its roots were not deep enough; its muscles had lost their vigour in the jog-trot of habit. Until the mind became once more a binding, personal responsibility, capable of making and following its own laws, until it once again recognized solitude as its hereditary element, our intellectual culture was merely a collection of habits, assumed and on certain occasions discarded with equal indifference.

Hesse gave most definite expression to his doubts about culture in an essay which appeared in 1919 and in which, proceeding from consideration of Dostoievsky's novel *The Karamasov Brothers*, he predicted the 'downfall of Europe': its downfall, but also its rebirth. According to Nietzsche, whose conception Hesse further develops in this essay, 'European Nihilism' consisted in the European's having surrounded himself with a multitude of equally valid

Cover of the first edition, designed by
K. E. Mende, 1919

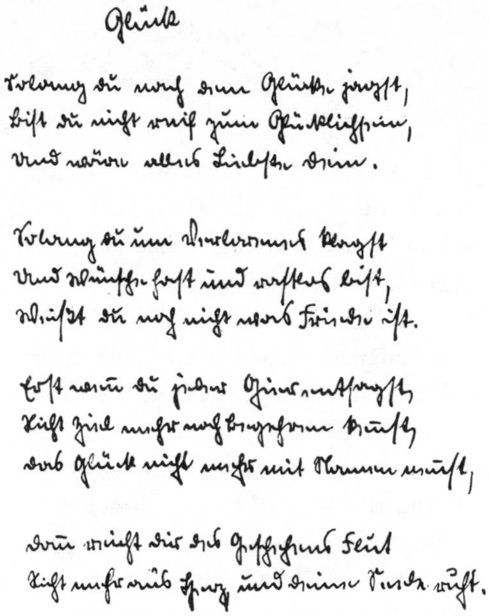

Glück

Solang du nach dem Glücke jagst,
Bist du nicht reif zum Glücklichsein,
Und wäre alles Liebste dein.

Solang du um Verlorenes klagst
Und Ziele hast und rastlos bist,
Weißt du noch nicht was Friede ist.

Erst wenn du jedem Wunsch entsagst,
Nicht Ziel mehr noch Begehren kennst,
Das Glück nicht mehr mit Namen nennst,

Dann reicht dir des Geschehens Flut
Nicht mehr ans Herz und deine Seele ruht.

Hermann Hesse's handwriting

Hesse's doubts with regard to culture

truths without associating them more closely with his own, personal life. In such circumstances the human mind becomes powerless to control and direct the irrational instincts that dwell in the deeper strata of the human soul and are dominant as motive force. Hesse foresees that European man will have to pass through unleashed chaos before he reaches the shore of the future, the new man. He will have to become familiar with all possibilities, including the criminal ones, in order to learn how to control them. He will have to brave the unchained fury of all existing forces before he can regain his mental integrity.

During the second world war there was a writer of Austrian descent living in Geneva — in voluntary exile like Hesse in the first world war — who, in an unfinished novel of which two parts had been published in 1930 and 1932, applied the touchstone to European culture. His name was Robert Musil and the title of his novel *Der Mann ohne Eigenschaften*. The name of Musil is also mentioned in the almanac to which we have referred. Like Hesse, Musil was alarmed to see all mental values swept away by a wave of newly-roused, primitive emotion at the outbreak of war. Being a sceptic, he realized that the same primitive emotion presumably existed among all peoples, which confirmed his assumption that the national label was attached subsequently. The existence of the emotion was undeniable, however. He described "how we are melted down by an unutterable feeling of humility in which the individual suddenly returns to the state in which he has no significance apart from his primitive task of protecting the clan". Musil also believes that at certain moments man experiences contact with a long-forgotten, primitive strata of emotion. But of what consequence are these isolated moments which allow him to escape from his individual attributes if he does not elaborate and define them with the critical methods of his century? Can one base a doctrine on a moment of purely personal experience? Is it not betraying our intellectual standards to set aside exact methods and sink into the arms of an irresponsible emotion? Yet, on the other hand, is it admissible simply to suppress the experience? Is this not to court a danger equally great, namely that the truths on which we are going to rely will be anonymous, separable, purely objective and devoid of any point of contact with our person at all?

Musil shared the conviction of Hesse that we shall have to pass through the chaos of indiscriminate qualities, of estranged and rootless cultural phenomena, in order to reach that other pole at which the world is revealed directly to the mind.

Or let us mention another name, this time not from the almanac.

Cover designed by Werner Rebhuhn

Page of Robert Musil's manuscript
'Der Mann ohne Eigenschaften'

Alfred Döblin
Charcoal drawing by Otto Pankok

Before the psychoanalytic doctrines of Freud, with which Hesse became acquainted at an early date as a patient, had become more widely known, Alfred Döblin, a neurologist practising in Berlin, was observing the seamy side of social progress in the rapidly growing city, as he treated patients who were suffering from what are now referred to as the diseases of civilization. In a series of articles Döblin described the typical cases which constantly appeared in different forms. In his best known novel, *Berlin Alexanderplatz*, he shows us life in a tenement house where the inmates of the different flats are captives of a fate which condemns them to loneliness and isolation. The bitterly hard years which Döblin had experienced in his youth, arriving in the city with his mother and smaller brothers and sisters, practically penniless, left their mark on his writings, and particularly in the novel he wrote as an emigrant, *Pardon wird nicht gegeben,* which is based on some of his early experiences. Döblin was one of the first to grasp the necessity of a new spiritual experience to match the constant extension of our range of consciousness due to technical and scientific progress. He saw the people of Berlin as atoms split off from an abandoned social order, coalescing to a mass, or remaining solitary only to be shattered by the blows of force. Whereas Hesse — and later Musil — divested civilized man of his personal characteristics by investigating to what extent these were still essential to him, Döblin, in *Berlin Alexanderplatz*, described the city-dweller who has lost his individuality, and in his Chinese story *Die Drei Sprünge des Wang-lun* the masses goaded on by the lash of hunger, greed and the desire

THOMAS MANN

INNEVARANDE ÅRS LITTERÄRA
NOBELPRIS, FÖRNÄMLIGAST FÖR
HANS STORA ROMAN BUDDEN-
BROOKS, VILKEN UNDER ÅRENS
LOPP VUNNIT ALLT MER STADGAT
ERKÄNNANDE SOM ETT AV DEN
SAMTIDA LITTERATURENS KLAS-
SISKA VERK

STOCKHOLM DEN 10 DECEMBER 1929

20
Robert Musil

2
Alfred Döbli

22
Walter
Hasenclever

2
Bertol
Brech

24   Ferdinand Bruckner »Die Verbrecher«, Schillertheater Berlin

for happiness, now following the lead of an individual, now spurned by him in favour of his solitude. In his novel *Wallenstein*, written during the first world war, Döblin depicts the great general of the Thirty Year's War as the blind instrument of historical destiny, while the counterpoise to his dynamic force is provided by the figure of the Emperor Ferdinand, who does not merely maintain his position and majesty as ruler, but when observed more closely reveals the unimpaired liberty, cold and clear, of individual consciousness. The paradox which might appear in the confrontation of these two characters does not exist for Döblin inasmuch as it is not the private ego of the ordinary person which he sees in the ego of the ruler — and of the writer — but the point of irruption of a supra-personal power: the daemonic element. When, as a result of relentlessly advancing technology, it becomes impossible to retain a private life; when the rich man only apparently does so through the material comforts with which he surrounds himself, while the poor man feels utterly abandoned, then, according to Döblin — who was influenced by Dostoyevsky, — it is time for human society, by a tremendous spiritual effort, to forge its way through to a new form of community life.

The big city and the tangible problem which it presents confronts the writer with an entirely new situation. It drew Robert Musil from Vienna to Berlin, where he gathered inspiration for his great novel *Der Mann ohne Eigenschaften*. Hermann Hesse, who was normally little concerned with urban matters, faced the question in his novel *Der Steppenwolf*. Thomas Mann never actually portrayed the big city but he captured something of the atmosphere of urban civilization in his novel *Der Zauberberg*. In Döblin's *Berlin Alexanderplatz* the voice of the city is heard directly.

One is tempted to ask why it was that, although a number of large cities existed in Europe before the first world war, Berlin only started to exert such a strong attraction on writers and artists after 1918. Observers from other countries, such as the Italian writer Corrado Alvaro, noticed that in Berlin interest was directed not so much towards the rest of Germany as towards Europe, if not towards the human race as a whole.

Italian and Russian futurism met in Berlin. The sense of abstract form suited the quick intellect of the city-dweller; it was saved from being reduced to

mere experimentation with forms by the expressive pathos which was encouraged by the Russian revolution. Towards the end of the 'twenties Corrado Alvaro wrote: "No one really knows how communism should be translated in terms of German values. Everyone, from the middle-class down to the working people, claps wildly at the theatre when they see a working man bring about the ruin of a member of the middle classes in a play on social emancipation." The fact that the German public saw in the revolution an outlet for suppressed feelings is altogether in keeping with the tendency of the German to overlook the social aspect and plunge directly into the universal one. Corrado Alvaro was also struck by the odd disproportion between the locally confined scene of the expressionist movement and its all-embracing vision of humanity. His Latin sense of proportion was offended by the sharp contrast between ordered precision, working discipline and technique on the one hand and on the other vague emphasis, Utopian ideas on humanity and emotional outbursts. He failed to understand that the two facets were mutually dependent, that the anonymous process which was constantly changing reality — most visibly in the city — also possessed an inner dimension and afforded the ego a view of the daemonic complexity of the unconscious.

The view of life appropriate to a denatured reality could no longer be made to fit an individual or citizen of a certain state. It had to rise up from strata of the soul in which slumbered the collective images of prehistoric times. There is nothing incompatible with this in the fact that at no other period has the ego been so passionately emphasized, so pathetically dramatized. While man as the engineer of reality divested himself of his private individuality, desiring at the same time to possess his experience intuitively, that is to say directly and unconditionally, the scene of this struggle for the attainment of a new man was the solitary, tormented and marooned ego of the modern European.

Berlin was not a historic city such as Vienna or Prague, but simply the typical big city which was considered to hold the future of man. Writers who had broken with their bourgeois origins — such as Bertolt Brecht, who came from Augsburg in the Swabian part of Bavaria — found a different atmosphere in Berlin than, for instance, in Munich, the other artistic centre of that period,

The city is the background against which the drama of the man of the future will unroll

which had a certain Bohemian tradition. Berlin was crueller and more radical. It raised no objections to experiments, but could also prove irritable, intolerant and sharply critical. Hugo von Hofmannsthal had to suffer as much under the authority of the critic Alfred Kerr (who favoured Gerhart Hauptmann's dramatic works) as did the young revolutionary Brecht.

Döblin used to declare — perhaps in a spirit of contradiction or because he was all too close to the theatre and business intrigues of Berlin — that better first nights were to be seen in the provinces. The statement implies that in general people looked to Berlin for manifestations of modern art.

In the plays of that period we are struck by the sharp contrast between excessive and often hysterical sentimentality and marked didactic intention. The intimate conflicts which the bourgeois age had concealed and which Ibsen had treated in his dramatic works, probing them in the light of a new morality, were now dragged out and relentlessly exposed. The revolt was not, or only indirectly, aimed at society, but rather at the father figure and paternal authority. The dramatic literature of the expressionists may be cited as the most convincing evidence in support of Ortega y Gasset's opinion that historical crises find their expression in the mutual relations between the members of the younger and the elder generation, who nominally share the same historical period but generally find that their common interests dwindle to a minimum in times of crisis. The revolt of the younger generation was introduced on the stage by Walter Hasenclever, Arnolt Bronnen and Fritz von Unruh, while Ferdinand Bruckner in *Die Verbrecher* and Peter Martin Lampel in *Revolte im Erziehungshaus* developed the theme in two plays which made a great stir. Revolt is a correlate of the intoxication of liberated vital consciousness, the pleasure in anarchy, but also of successful masculine fellowship. The generation is an association of contemporaries who have severed the bond which linked them to their fathers and are operating in unfamiliar country. Reminiscences from the fighting fronts are woven in. The town is not the familiar world of childhood but the stage on which the struggle for the future takes place. The atmosphere in Berlin was explosive during those years. Every political decision aggravated the latent crisis. Every attempt at effective planning led to the brink of civil war. It was, however, just this atmosphere simmering under the influence of

The artistic production of the expressionists

Walter Hasenclever
Drawing by Oskar Kokoschka

27

current affairs, which gave Berlin a start from which it advanced to become, artistically, the most up-to-date city in Europe. The spirit which was starting to penetrate the arts was as experimental as the prevailing political state of mind.

Young Brecht captured the spirit of the city on the battlefront of the future in his play *Trommeln in der Nacht*.

If we observe the situation more closely we notice that all the trends lead in one direction. The past, formerly the firm ground from which the new generation started out, had all of a sudden become useless because reality itself had lost its foot-hold, seeming to have only one dimension left: the future. In considering the literature of that period we must therefore take into account the change which had taken place in the contemporary mind. The belief that the past, or tradition, was handed on to us as a stable entity had been discarded as superstition. An almost exclusive emphasis was placed on the present, and everything that the past could offer had to be renovated and adapted to modern ideas. The present day was accepted unquestioningly as representing 'the zenith of time'. It was the tribunal before which the morals, fashions, views and beliefs of all times had to justify their existence. If a play by Goethe was produced, the question was not how the present time stood confrontation with Goethe, but on the contrary: how did Goethe stand up under the scrutiny of modern ideas. — All this with reference to a future which had been launched by the young generation and was not to be a mere visionary experience but was to be established as reality. Robert Musil published a series of essays entitled: *Versuche, den anderen Menschen zu finden*. Hermann Hesse spoke of the "incalculable being of the future". Alfred Döblin confronted both the bourgeois and the proletarian worlds with the existence of the 'daemonic', that is: man's inescapable urge towards the future.

The purpose of all these experiments was thus not just to alter social conditions, but to achieve a human being who should incorporate the change which, although for the time being still anonymous and not fully perceptible, had in reality already taken place. This mental image of the future could not be inferred from outward things but had to be found within the human soul. The self proved to be a permeable medium; the unity which was attributed to it in a determinable world turned out to be illusory. The majority of man's qualities were really qualities of the cultural environment in which he had been brought up. But these qualities could be detached from him.

It would seem that in periods when the cultural edifice starts to totter because people have ceased to believe in the former scale of values, man becomes conscious of his originally undefined nature. He feels himself no more than the site on which a multitude of tendencies meet and interact. He becomes aware of the foundations of his being sinking ever more deeply down to the original strata of pre-conscious life, over which his controlling experience has no power. He is only free in the dimension of the future. If the nature of his being is not clearly defined, then it is all the easier for him to determine what he shall be *Man as the task of the future* in the future. He can set in motion everything that he has ever been and that he discovers within himself, and with it trace out a possible future which will keep pace with the ever more rapidly materialising possibilities of technology.

Cover designed by G. Salter

The character of German literature

Conceptions are used in the interests of general comprehension. When we say 'German literature' what we mean for the moment is simply the subject of this essay. The expression is merely provisional, however, for the general conception which enters our minds when we hear the words 'German literature' will be progressively dispelled as we become more familiar with the matter we are investigating. German literature has, for instance, never attained the perfection of a system to the same degree as French literature, neither has it ever sought to achieve an independent system. To put it still more plainly: the sociable character of French literature has never existed in Germany but as an exception to the rule. A system can only evolve if the different elements to be embodied therein come to terms and subordinate their individual characteristics to a whole. This implies that interposed between the co-ordinating system and its multifarious manifestations there lies an intermediate zone in which the smooth transition of the individual element into a wider context is facilitated. It is no metaphor to speak of the social function of this intermediate zone, for the human being also is neither a mere cipher in a social system, nor on the other hand identical, as an individual, with his assigned role in society. Consideration of the *milieu* is, of course, required, but this does not exclude him from achieving individual recognition in his role and maintaining the position he has gained, without for that reason necessarily displaying egocentric obstinacy.

Stendhal's novel *Lucien Leuwen* describes a bourgeois *salon* which at the time of Louis Philippe vied with the aristocratic *salons* of the day as ambitiously as Madame Verdurin's vied with that of the Duchess of Guermantes in Proust's *A la Recherche du Temps Perdu*. One evening, in that rather insipid company, Lucien makes the acquaintance of a German scholar who, in spite of his youth,

German literature lacks the model character of a system

Attitude to society

possesses a vast range of knowledge in the field of comparative theology. However, it is precisely his ruthless exploitation of this universal erudition that makes a painful impression on the gathering, because he pours it out over his benumbed listeners without tact or restraint. The young man is so full of his own knowledge that he violates tacit taboos at every step and brutally refutes the weak objections raised by his hostess. His triumph as a scholar is his social defeat. By refusing to allow his listeners access to his knowledge he excludes himself from their company.

When a Frenchman wishes to define the form of a category of literature or the law which governs it he seeks to discover its exact position in a systematically ordered context: literature. The German inquires what is the essence of the poem, novel or short story. This type of question, going straight to the root of the phenomenon, does not contribute to systematism. Thus Stendhal's young scholar tacitly denies his hearers the right to any knowledge of their own because he has made such a thorough investigation of his subject. If we assume that he was aiming at a system, then this would have to be, first, universal, that is to say include all known manifestations of religion throughout the ages, and secondly the unity of the system could only be guaranteed by a greatness found in the depths of his own spirit. The middle region in which religions dwell, clothed in masks and vestments which depend on their native locality and in which they appear before the community, would presumably be left out of consideration.

There is a dream side to everything universal

This explains why in German literature we talk of classical verse forms, the classical drama or the classical form of novel in a different sense than do the French. The classical tragedy of Racine in its dramatic structure and metrical form not only represents the species according to the antique model but also reveals the social and moral character of seventeenth-century France. Goethe's *Iphigenie* on the other hand is the expression in classical form of purely human feelings, conflicts and aspirations which remain unaltered throughout the centuries.

The conception of classicism in German literature is not based on historical comparison but on a deeper level of experience

We have drawn this comparison in order to show at what point the voice of German literature is most likely to be heard in the concert of European cultural elements. Its stimulus is felt above all at times when the foundations of a previously stable order are beginning to crumble, when the necessity of deeper penetration into the problems of the time is felt, or when a system of vital beliefs becomes rigid and impermeable. We should, however, be cautious in applying the term 'revolutionary' to German literature.

The two great movements of modern German literature — 'storm and stress' and romanticism — did indeed take up arms against the mechanical principle underlying every order and strove to overthrow the barriers separating man from his real self; not, however, in order to replace the old order by a new one, but in order to enable the individual to partake unrestrictedly of what the world has to offer. The will to do away relentlessly with social conditions in which the individual is thwarted in his development or becomes the object of mechanised interests is revolutionary; the aspiration towards personal culture or the development of individual personality, taking precedence over the solution of the social problem, on the other hand, is counter-revolutionary. This modified interpretation of the revolutionary intention follows inevitably from the attitude of opposition to everything involved in the social community, when its members come to abhor the part which it forces them to play and every barrier between the freedom of the individual and the world as a whole becomes intolerable. This also explains why schools of thought or groups which unite in the struggle against a spurious order tend to part again just as rapidly, and why it is usually not the new community, or the new order, which justifies the zeal of the *avant-garde*, but personality with its own vital law. The revolutionary demand for change gives way to a desire for cultural transformation.

The result of this is that German literature does not, like the French, appear as an edifice complete in itself, although complex, built on traditional lines in accordance with ancient models, but rather as an area thickly strewn with ornaments, the pattern of which always points towards a hidden centre. This theoretical conclusion may be illustrated by a practical example. In France a particular form of literature is very often represented by the figure of the author who has most distinguished himself in that genre. The fable is La Fontaine's preserve, tragedy that of Corneille and Racine, comedy Molière's. Even the novel, since *La Princesse de Clève*, is accepted as the realm of Mme. de La Fayette. In Germany, on the other hand, the character of a literary work

In Germany, revolution is understood to imply not so much the improvement of conditions as the liberation of the individual's personality

In France the writer often represents a particular literary species

32

lies not so much in its form as in the personal and biographical aspect. In France one may hear the opinion that Goethe's personality was greater than his works. Maurice Barrès, for instance, wrote: "In our eyes his merit lies in the superbly disciplined conduct of his life... His works are of secondary importance." The German feels just the opposite. We tend to call a literary work which is so completely a 'work', or 'opus', that it overshadows its author, cold or artificial, finding it lacking in the confessional aspect which reveals itself in German lyric poetry, character novels and even dramatic works. The anti-social trait found in the works of Jean-Jacques Rousseau, his belief in an original or primary state, of a universal nature, which must be rediscovered, explains the exemplary influence which he exerted on Herder, the young Goethe and Jean Paul. The 'primary' takes first place in our aesthetics; 'originality' is not quite the same. A work is 'original' by comparison with others. The original in the sense of the primary, however, is a breaking out, an escape to freedom, as the captive bursts his fetters and escapes in the oldest literary monument of our language, the second *Merseburger Zauberspruch*. And since freedom is not only the bursting of chains but the transition to a state which, as opposed to captivity, is the real and original state, the primary bears the hallmark of genuineness, being that which is revealed as the pure and absolute substance of being when the concealing veil is withdrawn.

It is hard to reconcile the classification of the primary as the highest order of poetic and artistic production with a literary or aesthetic system, and literary criticism in Germany has always suffered from this disadvantage. If we judge a writer by how great a contribution he has made, not towards the enrichment of literature, but to its system, the false impression may be given that the work itself is unimportant as a literary document once the personal element has been detached from it. If, on the other hand, we judge a writer by the degree to which his work testifies to primary intensity, that is in how far it is unmistakable and hence genuine, the equally false impression may result that the elaboration of literary forms and themes or the development of existing models indicates a lack of creative genius. Ernst Robert Curtius distinguished between creative and elaborative periods in literature. We could go a step further and state that the creative and the elaborative principle in literature constantly alternate and neither can

In Germany a species may personify an eternal, human type

The 'original' and the 'primary'

The alternating principle

33

exist without the other. For primary creative genius, without elaboration, sweeps over forms like a forest fire, destroying them through intensified brilliance, whereas elaboration devoid of the primary spark has only the laurels of the past to offer.

Education and Adventure

There are a number of German folk-tales which relate the adventures of one who sets out from home to seek his fortune. Quite often it is the most unpretentious of several brothers who finally marries the princess. Sometimes he is the youngest, the mother's darling, who has no special talents, but while roaming through the woods has learnt the language of the birds and made friends with dwarfs and spirits who later come to his aid when he is in danger. His rough brothers, who at first glance appear far more capable of mastering the problems and trials of life, come home having achieved nothing. The youngest, however, who has always been considered a good-for-nothing, to the astonishment of all carries away the prize.

Folk-tales can be interpreted in many different ways, but never completely fathomed. The story of the good-for-nothing, however, teaches us that in the realm of the folk-tale it is precisely the individual who appears to be a misfit in the world who is destined to rise to the greatest heights. Just because he possesses no outstanding quality, neither physical strength nor unusual intelligence, he is capable of participating in all things and attaining the greatest wisdom. Thus he who in the practical eyes of his fellows is a misfit in the world because he does not wear the badge of a trade, is in a deeper sense the only one who is really at home in it. The world lays its treasures at his feet and renders hommage to him as a prince.

For the German, education in the broader sense means the progress of the individual towards unlimited participation in the world, and when we rebel against the constraint of fashion and the artificiality of convention we do this not so much in favour of better habits and a more sensible way of life as with a view to that universal participation in which the individual passes beyond all barriers to apprehend the whole and thus to achieve his own fullest development.

The folk-tale contains a naïve expression of this idea. In the German *Bildungs-roman*, which describes the personal development and progress of a particular character and may thus be referred to as a character novel, the inconspicuous hero, with his lack of any outstanding feature or talent, is the prototype of the species. Christoph von Grimmelshausen's *Simplicius Simplicissimus* is a folk-tale hero who, in contrast to his Spanish counterpart the picaroon, or rogue, possesses not only worldly wisdom but also depth of feeling. In Jean Paul's most important work, *Titan*, the hero is a youth whose harmonious nature prevails against the strongest wills, the intellectual giants, the passionate and the sensitive natures, like the steady radiance of the sun. Goethe's *Wilhelm Meister* is neither gifted nor enterprising, but with his sincere sympathy, kindness and helpfulness, his reticence in passing judgment and his sense of justice, he contrives to do the right thing wherever he goes, and in so doing gains the sympathy and support of occult powers. His greatest virtue is that he is true to himself. This teaches him to discriminate between the fitting and the unfitting, to adapt for himself what suits his nature and pass over what is foreign to him without prejudice or condemnation.

In order satisfactorily to study the problem of the modern German novel it is essential to take a look at its classical predecessor, examples of which are *Der Grüne Heinrich* by the Swiss author, Gottfried Keller, and *Der Nachsommer* by the Austrian, Adalbert Stifter. It becomes evident that the former character novel reappears in Thomas Mann's *Der Zauberberg* and in *Die Bekenntnisse des Hoch-staplers Felix Krull*, but with an ironic turn, while in the trilogy *Die Schlaf-wandler* by Hermann Broch, the every-day man is no more than a mechanically adapted particle in relation to his environment and the irrational forces which could have developed his mind no longer succeed in rising to the surface of his consciousness. Thus he is sleep-walking in a double sense: on the one hand as representative of the specialized, purposeful, sober activity of the professional man, and on the other as the plaything of irrational forces. The intersection cuts across what were formerly the two essential components of education: knowledge and its application. Hans Castorp in Thomas Mann's novel, while staying as a patient in the sanatorium at Davos, acquires a great deal of know-ledge but cannot apply it in an appropriately active life, merely existing as he does in the half anonymous and half luxurious state of illness, which bears a

38
Rainer Maria
Rilke

3
Fra
Kafl

udolf Alexander
hröder

Ernst
Jünger

Gerhart Hauptmann/
Eugene O'Neill

Hugo von Hofmannsthal

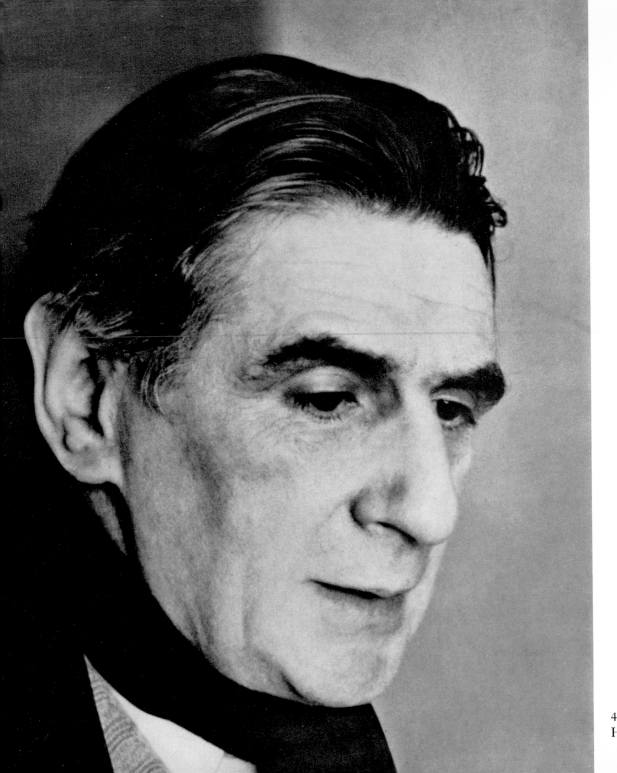

44
Hermann Broch

Vorderhand das Motto, das den Inhalt umreisst

(verzeihen Sie, dass es gereimt ist)

Fühl ich das Staunen? staunt mein Ich?
Von welche Grenze kommst du her
Gedanken, tiefstes Ungefähr!
Im Todesraume schwebe ich,
Schreiend und ewig, Ahasver —

Gemeint die Angst, die aus der Spalte zwischen dem
„ich denke" und dem „es denkt" immer hervorbricht,
die „philosophische Angst", die sich letzten Endes
doch nur am platonischen „ich denke" beruhigen
kann — das Logische im Ethischen

Hermann Broch's handwriting

certain similarity to the somnolescent progress of Broch's sleep-walkers. *Der Zauberberg* and *Die Schlafwandler* are a mixture of the society novel and the character novel. The tradition of the German character novel — right back to the picaresque story and the folk-tale of *Lucky Hans* — finds its purest expression in Hermann Hesse, who through the fiction of the romantic period has genuine contact with the myth. In Hesse too, however, the former unconstrained relationship to the world has been split into conflicting elements. Education appears to be no longer effective unless it originates in those depths, or that region of direct perception, which knowledge itself denies us. *Demian* is the youthful

Cover-design by Werner Rebhuhn

embodiment of the 'daemonic' force which — as we learnt from Döblin — is to liberate man from his egoistic and self-righteous shell. — But can we set a limit to the daemonic? Does it not multiply and disintegrate our inner life to infinity, unless the mind is capable of reintegrating us in the contemplation of ourselves? Hesse always stressed that the ideal he had in mind was the symbolic unity of both tendencies, and when following the fate of his restless, 'daemonic' figures the reader should not forget the others of collected and temperate mind. He also pointed out in his defence that in the face of present-day reality education could no longer be clearly defined but only regarded as something moving to and fro between opposite poles.

Works in which the process of education still appears to proceed in the traditional manner are either retrospective in character — as for instance Werner Bergengruen's *Der letzte Rittmeister* — or romantic fantasies such as the charming story *Squirrel* by Ernst Penzoldt.

Education has a verbal rather than a substantival meaning

Let us remember, however, that in the classical German novel education also had a verbal rather than a substantival meaning. It was acquired in adventurous circumstances and introduced the hero to mysterious regions. To seek education also means to appear before a court which passes impartial judgment on our capabilities and our character. Seen in this light, the ex-convict Franz Biberkopf in Döblin's *Berlin Alexanderplatz,* who grapples with the world and in the end has to sacrifice his stubborn ego, is also a seeker who learns from the world like Goethe's Faust.

German literature comes to the fore in times of crisis

German literature generally comes to the fore at times when an established system is losing its authority and the social order is crumbling. For in such times of historical crisis the individual is left unprotected and with only himself to rely on, in face of a reality the eternally elusive strangeness of which has hitherto been hidden from him by a barrier of institutions, customs and rules of behaviour. At those moments the radical problems inherent in the German conception of education become of topical interest. It is significant that in France, when Goethe's name is mentioned, people immediately think of *Die Leiden des jungen Werther* and *Faust*, not of *Iphigenie* or *Die Wahlverwandtschaften*. For it is not that with which we are familiar at home which we find stimulating, but the unwonted, the exotic. The generation of Spanish writers

46

which took its name from the fateful year 1898 became a centre of interest in other countries when it risked a venture which was in keeping with the times but which could not develop so freely elsewhere, being obstructed by the prevailing level of civilization. At about the same time as Spain entered the European scene: when the writings of Ortega y Gasset and Miguel de Unamuno began to be generally read on the continent; when Velazquez and El Greco, Picasso and Juan Gris became familiar topics of discussion; when Henry de Montherlant analysed the aesthetic experience of Maurice Barrès in Spain and prepared for a direct encounter with Spanish influences — not as an impersonal onlooker behind the barrier, but right in the arena, at that moment German literature also began to attract renewed attention.

The two main features of Friedrich Nietzsche's philosophy were a radical scepticism in face of all traditional moral concepts and a strong emphasis on the vital will. The two go together: nihilism and belief in life, psychological exposure and dithyrambic exuberance. The conviction that the hidden interests of some power underly all moral concepts is acquired by a psychological process. Nietzsche's unquestioning confidence in psychology which penetrates into every corner of the soul, revealing and unmasking hidden motives, was entirely in harmony with the nineteenth century's faith in science. His drastic innovation appears in his rejection of the scientific ideal of truth in favour of the reality of life as supreme criterion. By placing psychology at the service of the will, Nietzsche transforms it from a method of perception into an instrument for the higher education of man. His philosophy is the hammer with which he shatters the tables of traditional moral criteria; it is the liberating tool which releases the minds of men from the fetters of prejudice, from atrophied notions of good and evil, from withered virtues revealing only lost vitality, to restore them after long captivity to the original untamed state of real life. It is clear that this heroic will to achieve supreme liberty is born of despair over the traditional values of civilization. The phenomenon of European nihilism is the expression of this despair; nihilism because certain values are still ostensibly accepted but no longer exert an active influence on life and are merely carried along passively as ballast. Nietzsche's criticism is not directed against the values as such, but against the sickness and fatigue of a civilization which is no longer capable

The dual aspect of Nietzsche's philosophy

The European suffers from the knowledge of too many truths; this is the source of European nihilism

of creating new values and is subservient to a cowardly, deceitful or falsely aestheticized morality.

The radical process of psychological exposure by which Nietzsche tracks down the secret motives and hidden interests involved in religion and morality, in the soul of the artist, the writer and the philosopher, and reveals their false practices, is not pursued in the name of truth but in the name of personal sincerity. The distinction is important inasmuch as not only philosophy but also art thus re-enters the realm of personal responsibility. Nietzsche does not aim at the determination of psychological truths in the sense of scientific knowledge, but at liberating man from his illusions, overcoming moral dishonesty, and achieving a higher development of the individual, for whom all former values are superseded because he has reached a state of maturity in which he is able himself to create new values.

The marked influence which Nietzsche had on his age is explained by the new

Friedrich Nietzsche's handwriting

48

ethos of life which is evident in his philosophy. With psychology preparing the way as an ally, this ethos casts off all remaining dross and is revealed in its essence as pure, personal will. Nietzsche's successors subsequently developed two different attitudes which are related and of which neither can exist without the other: the attitude of the critical observer who dissociates himself from current opinions and ideas, rejecting them as a hollow sham, because only genuinely lived life activates the personal ethos; and on the other hand the ecstatic attitude, divesting man of his self for the sake of the unimpaired totality of life, which is inevitably diminished by our moral rules and ideas.

Whereas the observer assures himself of a freedom distinguished by self-denial, the ecstatic assures himself of a freedom which is to consist in unlimited participation.

Here we may recognize two tendencies which form a part of the basic concept of education and the character novel: to discredit the interests — in whatever form they may appear — which society foists upon the individual in the guise of morality, or, on the other hand, to lay exclusive emphasis on the inner urge which through active and creative development brings man into direct contact with the whole of life.

The meaning of the word 'education', however, has undergone an important change since Nietzsche's time. In the nineteenth century, education and knowledge were more or less synonymous. During the second half of the century, however, the conception of education which had formerly been universal became slightly restricted as certain kinds of knowledge were developed which no longer automatically fell within its province. The natural sciences were still regarded as widening the educational horizon as well as that of knowledge, although a discrepancy could already be observed between the humanitarian view of the world held by the arts and the rational view held by science, with regard to their relative accessibility for the individual. Technical knowledge, however, could no longer be reconciled with the original notion of education. It found expression in the physical control of material forces and objects; it harnessed energies and altered the familiar world without any apparent benefit to the personal culture of the individual. The second factor which raised doubts as to the distant possibility of universal education was the awakening of the masses,

Nietzsche's moral claim

Friedrich Nietzsche Drawing by Lieder

Technology and the masses are complementary. Both are distinguished by the absence of fixed characteristics

49

The epicurean attitude towards culture

The notion of education radically transformed in Nietzsche's philosophy

which had introduced a dangerous element of instability into the play of social forces, as a result of which it was no longer quite certain that the validity of the earlier conception of 'education' could still be taken for granted. Thus in the introduction to his novel *Lucien Leuwen*, Stendhal suggests an alternative which would place education at the discretion of the individual, depending on his personal inclination. For while political necessity may indeed favour the victory of the democratic idea, cultivated taste will prefer the intellectual refinement of the *ancien régime*.

This means that however desirable the social justice promised by a democratic regime may be, to live under such a regime is, for the educated person, equally undesirable. The ugly picture which Stendhal sees resulting from a complete victory of the democratic idea reveals totalitarian traits, perhaps inspired by the tyranny of Robespierre. However, in expressing his aversion for the democratic regime and his preference for a corrupt system which allows him to enjoy the pleasures of cultured intercourse and follow his own inclinations, he invests education with an aesthetic or epicurean title. It becomes antagonistic to the forces which are responsible for and determine the progressive alteration of the world. Education becomes a privilege, deriving its title from the privileged class and, in the eyes of the masses, occupying its own preserve.

Nietzsche resists this restriction of the educational horizon by making of thought a tool in the service of the will. Although he also regards the advance of the democratic idea as a symptom of decadence and as a free spirit takes an aristocratic standpoint, the fact that he suffers from European nihilism leaves him no other choice than to take the rising forces into account as expressions of will, when considering the development of the future.

We have sketched the main lines of the revolutionary transformation which the conception of education underwent in Nietzsche's philosophy. When education is no longer identical with contemporary knowledge, when for instance the knowledge of history is regarded as a disadvantage rather than an advantage, because too much historical knowledge cripples the creative power and adulterates the historical perception of the present by introducing an infinite relativism, then the question arises: If it no longer corresponds to knowledge, where should genuine education start?

If we remember that the two aspects which had come to dominate the aesthetics of art since the romantic period were the primary character of intuition and the progressive intensification of artistic forms, then it becomes clear to us why the ideas of Nietzsche had such a lasting influence particularly on artists. What had hitherto been valid in the aesthetic realm was now to be a rule of conduct for the elite. The intellect was to accept its paradoxical nature and proceed in both directions at the cross-roads, allowing neither ecclesiastical nor worldly authority to curb its impetus, obedient only to its inner necessity and following the daemon of will to the most distant horizons.

Application of aesthetic principles of conduct to an elite

The dual nature of Nietzsche's philosophy became even more evident in his successors than in his own case. On the one hand he had begotten a morality which was adapted to the alternating rhythm of life, constantly moving between opposite poles, solitude and sociability, asceticism and sensualism, strictest discipline and roving adventure. Here his disciples were Hermann Hesse, Thomas Mann and Gottfried Benn.

Duality of Nietzsche's successors

On the other hand he was celebrated as the founder of irrational mysteries. His name was invoked as the advocate of the primitive awe which is hostile to the intellect, as prophet of the renegade vital force. In this context may be mentioned Oswald Spengler, Ludwig Klages and in a certain respect also Ernst Jünger. Thus among Nietzsche's successors we find two definitely conflicting tendencies: ironic scepsis prepared for every mental adventure, and a determination to indulge

English edition. 'Auf den Marmorklippen'

in the irrational. The explanation of this strange contradiction is as follows: Nietzsche made the morality of the artist into the morality of the free spirit *par excellence*, in which life itself occupied the place of the work of art. The artistic, creative process is distinguished by the alternation of imagination and criticism, inspiration and elaboration, which become polarized in the work during the creative process. If the work is lacking as point of reference and the elements mentioned become independent factors in the free conduct of life, then polarization can no longer take place. Intuition seeks an idea by which the world may once more be revealed to man's consciousness as a whole; criticism regards forms and symbols as the only solid ground for the mind and attributes to it a purely associational function.

In transition periods style becomes a vehicle of self-discovery

In the dynamic epochs of literature the flood-gates are raised between literature as a system and reality. The author is no longer content to remain within the prescribed limits of a literary species or conform to a style, rule or agreement previously established. He does not feel that he has really embarked on his mission until he reaches the point where tradition and habit in writing forsake him. He can only discover what is required of him through direct contact with real things. Rousseau, in his *Confessions*, did not fail to mention insignificant and mortifying details of his life as well. He refused to submit to any rule of literary decorum which would have impaired the sincerity of his writing by differentiation between the 'decent' and the 'indecent'. He wanted to write in the style which would correspond most closely to his own temperament. In doing so he challenged the current system of literature by his style of writing and his manner of direct presentation. His book left the impression that nothing written before had ever been fully sincere, or at least that it was no longer permissible to write in accordance with the long accepted practice and rule.

Nietzsche's criticism of accepted values

A similar impulse emanated from Nietzsche's works. His purpose in revising all values was to point out the questionable nature of what was accepted as self-evident; questionable in view of the fact that on closer examination what was imagined to be a vitally necessary support frequently turned out, on the contrary, to be an obstacle.

In the nineteenth century people had become used to entrusting reality to the organized sciences and accepting what the latter decreed to be the truth as binding in the sphere of their personal lives. Nietzsche introduced a spirit of doubt as to the infallibility of recognized conceptions. That which is valid within a particular system, in so far as it contributes to it as a clearly defined conception, may reveal itself outside that system as something which has been indefinable and unknown since time immemorial. Thus, for instance, in view of reality outside the sphere of science the question of where man really belongs still demands an answer. If anything can teach him about his own nature and his rightful place it is the probings of his own mind. This implies the mental effort of breaking away from the confines of established knowledge to set up outposts in a realm still unexplored by conceptual thought. Man relies on his own powers to decide where his future spiritual home shall be, looking out from the shores of the continent which has outlawed him for a new world.

Man will decide his own future place in the world

Handwriting of Ernst Jünger
from the preface to the new French
translation of 'In Stahlgewittern' (1960)

The poet's mission

Aesthetic autonomy allows a reintegration of the poetic

It may be concluded from the foregoing that in Germany lyric poetry occupies a favoured position. In it the vital consciousness of a new generation first becomes directly manifest, turning to the theatre in the second place and only then to the novel. The fate of lyric poetry in the nineteenth century was the same as that of all forms of intellectual expression which did not proceed with a steady methodical gait. Looking through the popular anthologies of the period it is easy to see where poetry still found a place in man's strictly run domestic life. As nature poetry it was a source of recreation for leisure hours and holidays; it offered the comfort and good counsel which could no longer be drawn so directly from religion and science; within the restricted sphere of education it bore witness to truth and beauty and noble qualities, which through no fault of their own were gradually falling into aesthetic isolation.

The aesthete has been scorned and represented as a parasite of conventional society. Yet it was aesthetic sensibility which fostered the thought that poetry as well as art possessed a truth of its own which was beyond comparison with any truth discovered by scientific methods. It was therefore not correct to say that as science and technical progress invaded ever greater areas of reality the artist was left with no choice but to withdraw into his own world of dreams. On the contrary, the refined aesthetic sensibility of the artist or poet led him to direct his attention away from himself to the special type of work, the methods and the means by which artistic production is made possible at all.

What distinguished this work from any other was the fact that in this case there was no universally binding method which led to a universally accepted result, but method and production were inseparably merged and expressed truth in a form which, although bearing an individual stamp, was understood as truth of a personal nature. It was the purely aesthetic attitude, devoid of all purpose, which inspired the new doctrine that a work of art spoke its own language and could not be otherwise defined in words; that it must resist all attempts made to attribute intentions or purposes to it and conform strictly to the laws of its own domain; that at the same time, however, no limits were imposed on the artistic sense or any other perceptive faculty, leaving it free to embrace the whole of reality; all the more so while men were eagerly submitting both at work and at leisure to the ruling forces of the time: the natural sciences and technical progress. In general, aesthetic contemplation transfers its object into a region untouched by the transitory nature of human life. In his famous ode, John Keats apostrophizes the nightingale: "Immortal bird". The immortality of the beautiful appears, as Platonic idea, in contrast to the shadow-like passage and decay of human life. The reversal of this situation which occurs in Oscar Wilde's novel *The portrait of Dorian Gray*, when the traces of age and vice appear in the portrait while the young man it portrays enjoys lasting youth, at first appears as merely an ingenious idea. However, a smart idea may often sum up a whole course of development. More important than the inversion making youth and beauty last while the work of art decays is the fact that time has been introduced into the relation of the two; the work of art is deprived of its timeless aspect and made to compare with earthly life. In this is expressed what man now expects of art, it is no longer to be the timeless image of an idea, but on the contrary to express moments of intense experience, no longer to occupy its own domain apart from the temporal existence of man but to be a concentrated extract of reality, that reality which he can experience directly within himself. Thus art ceases to exist as an objective sphere of its own. The life of art depends on the spirit of the times, and this, although it has its source in the experience of the individual, yet possesses the miraculous faculty of embracing time in all its forms.

The nightingale as idea and as poetic image

Immediate, topical experience has replaced the timeless idea

Aesthetic contemplation is also the receptive sense which allows the new spirit of the times to become manifest. If I look at the intricate design of a carpet I am first of all conscious of the carpet as an object. I gaze at it with pleasure and call it beautiful. I may go no further than this opinion; my relation to the carpet may remain quite simple. It may also happen, though, that I read myself into the pattern on the carpet and discover in the multitude of interwoven lines an image of infinity — passing from my normal, unidimensional time into a labyrinthine time. In this case the carpet no longer exists independently of me as an object, neither is my own attitude towards it completely impartial; my relationship to it becomes one of progressive realization in which I advance along a path which now leads me to the heights of complete identification with the pattern, only to plunge down again into the depths of estrangement, without ever allowing me to grasp the pattern as a whole.

The rhythm of personal experience which I have illustrated above is characteristic of lyric poetry in the period of which we are writing. The aesthetic trait is unmistakable. It marks the first volumes of Stefan George's poems and lends the poems and smaller plays of Hugo von Hofmannsthal their delicate bloom. It is the background against which Rilke's receptivity places things. In accordance with the different dispositions of the three poets mentioned, the aesthetic theme appears in a different role in each case, on the side of the protagonist or on that of the antagonist. If we grasp the paradox involved in the fact that time leaves behind an image which appears for one moment in its restless course, we have a key to the understanding of the lyric poetry of that time. The image stands in space; yet space estranges it from time which is the only guarantee of its durability. If we wish to translate space into time or to represent time as space we are obliged, in order to bridge the interval between them, to make use of numbers.

Stefan George's volume of poems: *Der Siebente Ring* is based on a numerical system. If we observe the relationship between architecture and music which Paul Valéry described in his dialogue *Eupalinos* and which, in virtue of the function of number and proportion, appears on the one hand to organize the spatial aspect and on the other the temporal, it is only logical that George, in order to materialize his poem in space, dissociates it from every other verbal form, individualizes it even down to the typography and stresses its unique value in exquisitely got-up editions. The unmistakable and irreplaceable character in which lies the value of a work of art finds a temporal equivalent in those moments which seem to rise above the passage of time to bestow an experience of eternal value. Spatial and temporal experience alternate in George's poems. One volume is entitled *Der Teppich des Lebens*, another *Das Jahr der Seele*. One poem

Title page designed by
Melchior Lechter, 1907

describes the autumn scenery in a park, and in the last line we are exhorted to listen to the dull thud of ripe fruit falling to the ground. This knocking of the waning year at the threshold of the underworld, with the unexpected transition from visual to aural perception, is reminiscent of Baudelaire's poem in *Les Fleurs du Mal*, in which a vision of luminous, late-summer days is interrupted by the crash of logs on the paving of the courtyard, conjuring up the idea of a gallows being prepared for the year which has run its course.

George, who translated Baudelaire's *Fleurs du Mal* and was akin to Mallarmé in his pursuit of an ideal of purity of poetic expression, devoted the whole force of his powerful personality to the task of purging poetry of all trivial language and hackneyed phrases. Like Mallarmé, he drew a dividing line right through the language, separating the vocabulary used merely for imparting information and for mutual understanding from the language appropriate to poetic expression. He distinguished between elevated language and ordinary language. He accepted the fetters which his ideal imposed, as well as the accusation of preciosity which was levelled at him, rather than abandon an inch of ground in his claim that art should exercise the strictest restraint in face of everything commonplace.

Stefan George
Woodcut by Reinhold Lepsius

Solches bleibt nunmehr zu tun:
Schritte die dein blick Gegriff
Innen als ein wunder sehn.

Handwriting of Stefan George

All elevated language, however — be it the language of Dante in the *Divina Commedia*, of Milton in *Paradise Lost* or of Klopstock in the biblical epic *Messias* — is the expression of a still higher, supreme word. Goethe's Faust also ponders over the word, the *logos*, and is in doubt as to which came first: conscious being or creative action. In George's works the elevated language has, so to speak, no higher agency above it. Yet it still has a mission to fulfil and celebrates exalted moments of existence, exalted incarnations of history. Yet these heights can only be justified by the height to which the author of the word has climbed as judge condemning the shortcomings of his time and as pioneer of new values. The aestheticism originally underlying George's poetry deprives his works, however exalted they are, and however great their influence upon his age, of the necessary stable foundation, so that in the eyes of his successors they appear as a rather shaky edifice.

Hugo von Hofmannsthal

The situation is different in the case of Hugo von Hofmannsthal. If, as we stated at the beginning of this chapter, poetic activity has liberated itself from all standards of comparison and only seeks to achieve its own truth — poetic truth — then we too cannot judge it by any other criterion than the extent of its own energy and intensity. In doing so we shall notice that there are two types of creative artist, of which one is distinguished by his active nature while the other is more of a medium. The first type tends towards constructive and futuristic action; the second is receptive for the influences of his time, empathetic and deeply imbued with memories. We shall revert to this differentiation when considering the novel of the nineteen-twenties.

A reminiscent trend which is constructive, futuristic and mediumistic

If we say that Hofmannsthal, in contrast to George, personifies the medium-istic type, we must immediately add that in doing so we also stamp him as an Austrian poet. The Habsburg Empire, which was becoming ever more unreal as a genuine ruling power in the period before the first world war, paralysed as it was by bureaucratic abstraction and risking loss of authority no less when seeking conciliatory settlements within its frontiers than in the exercise of violence, increased in importance as a contemporary and historical principle of order in the same measure as its outward significance waned. Hardly one of the outstanding Austrian poets who have contributed so much to German literature in our century remained untouched by this historic, imperial conception. Its influence is even traceable in the active or futuristic ideas of Robert Musil, this being, incidentally, the only possible explanation of the analogy to be found between his *Mann ohne Eigenschaften* and Proust's *A la Recherche du Temps Perdu. Der Tod des Vergil* by Hermann Broch, a work portraying the eternal cycle of growth and decay, is inconceivable without the idea of an invisible and yet ever-present empire in the background. In Franz Kafka's novels we are

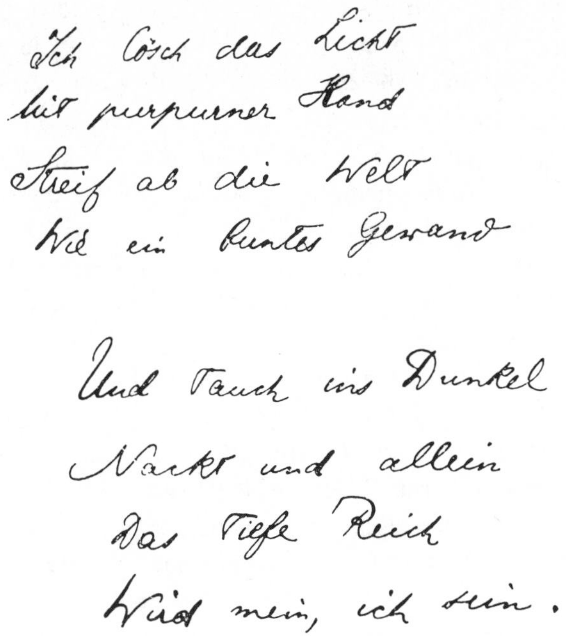

Ich lösch das Licht
Mit purpurner Hand
Streif ab die Welt
Wie ein buntes Gewand

Und tauch ins Dunkel
Nackt und allein
Das Tiefe Reich
Wird mein, ich sein.

Handwriting of Hugo von Hofmannsthal

alarmed to feel a massive universal structure closing in from all sides so that time is short. In his poetry, Hofmannsthal is the spiritual heir to this empire. The motif which is common to his poems and lyric plays is precisely the moment — in his plays the meeting — which promises ultimate revelation of the fundamental unity of the world while simultaneously casting the ominous shadow of fate. In his poem *Nox portentis gravida* it is the ominous cloud covering a third of the night sky. In the one-act play *Die Frau im Fenster* violent death approaches Dianora from behind at the very moment in which her heart opens to embrace the whole world. Claudio in *Der Tor und der Tod* recognizes the reality he has always failed to grasp only when he is deprived of it for ever. The premonition that, beyond all its infinite complexity, the world still remains a

Cover 1898

The creative, cultural mission of Rudolf Borchardt

mysteriously interwoven whole, a unity, a universe turned away towards the night, underlies all of Hofmannsthal's poetry. If this conception of the world is true, however, it immediately raises the question of whether personal experience is adequate to substantiate this truth. The poet who accepts this truth as his fate is condemned from then on to live on the furthest outskirts of the world as it has become: banished and nameless, a stranger in his own land, discerning in everything he sees the ugly scar of former associations.

The sanctuary of art, which George had proudly and defiantly set up in the world, was developed by Hofmannsthal as an inward universe. For him the magic key of poetry opened the gates to all periods of history. He saw the origin of the poet's mission in the limitations and the need of a humanity which can no longer believe, which finds no help in knowledge, and which thirsts after poetry as the last source of living truth. The poet's neediness, when his only hope of encountering the truth he is seeking lies outside the world in the realm of language, and the eternal call of mankind for poetry, are complementary and form the basis of the poet's brotherly mission. This means, however, that the individual poet is not so important as poetry itself, his personal style of less interest than the language of poetry in general. The mandate which the poet derives from his gift is not exclusively in his name. It is granted him in the name of poetry, and if he makes good use of it he can restore to the world something which it has lost in the course of the ages. Hofmannsthal drew inspiration from sources which are named in the history of literature: from the comedies of Molière, the *comedia* of Calderon, the fairy-tale operas of Raimund, all of which were nourished from the same subterranean lode. His delicate feeling for language and theatrical versatility enabled Hofmannsthal to reveal the transparent essence of every form and colour it with his own spirit. While he appears to withdraw into the background as poet, poetry itself appears, through him, in a sublimated form.

This aim he shared with George who also endeavoured, in a period of linguistic decadence, to show his countrymen what great poetry had once been like in the literature of their country. The third companion in arms was Rudolf Borchardt, whose relations with George were extremely strained, but never with regard to the common cause to which all three felt bound. Even Hofmannsthal could not always satisfy the demands of Borchardt, who expected the will to achieve what in the poet springs spontaneously from his talent. The full scope of Borchardt's constructive criticism, which embraced all aspects of culture and was based on the poetic ideal, to which history also is indebted for its truth, has not yet been appreciated. In contrast to Hofmannsthal, who had the gift of poetic integration, Borchardt made his brilliant mastery of language serve a purpose which always overshadowed the literary work. When he took a play like Carlo Goldoni's *Pamela* and, as it were, translated it back into the original form of Richardson's novel, he did so not only to create a part worthy of a famous actress of the time but also to read his contemporaries a lecture on the English gentleman's conception of honour, and to attack the wrong attitude of the socialists. In other words the importance of the work itself is always secondary to the purpose Borchardt intends it to fulfil. It does not possess the ingenuous, natural quality of poetic creation but rather the premeditated effect of masterly skill; it is the illustration of an argument, evidence in support of a theory. If we take this aspect into account and recognize Borchardt's works as an impressive, if presumptuous attempt to reconstruct the entire edifice of poetry like an antique temple, we may dimly guess how he visualized the completion of his audacious plan.

Rudolf Alexander Schröder was a friend of Hofmannsthal's and Borchardt's. His contribution to their great project for the revival of poetry was to make our classical heritage reaccessible in up-to-date language. He translated the Odyssey and later the Iliad into a metre more natural to the German language than classical hexameters, and replaced the stilted wording of earlier translations by vigorous, original language. He translated the poems of Horace, Virgil's Bucolics, the Georgics and the Aeniad in a concise and pithy style which has seldom been equalled in German versions of a Latin original. French tragedy, the comedies of Molière and also Shakespearian drama tempted Schröder, following the example of the Schlegel brothers, to prove that the German language is ideally suited for translations.

*Rudolf Alexander Schröder –
the universal language of poetry*

In his own poetry Schröder subdues the subjective element in favour of form. In contrast to Borchardt, with whom every poetic theme becomes the centre of interests which radiate in all directions, Schröder is a poet in the original sense of the word: a maker and artisan of language, whom no outside interest

Klassische Ode.

Ich bin gewesen, wo ich schon einmal war:
Mai und der Juni waren mein Weggeleit;
  An ihren Händen bin ich wieder
  Zwischen die Hügel hinein gekommen,

Und kannte fast die Wege nicht mehr! Doch gieng
Mir untern Füssen, – wie sich durch Morgen-Rauch
  Der Bau der Landschaft unerschüttert
  Gegen den scheinbaren Aufruhr herstellt –,

Der Trost der sichern Erde im Herzen auf:
Denn es bewölkt das Himmlische Teil in uns
  Das irdische mit seiner Schöpfung,
  Eh es uns Tagt; und es tagt nicht jedem. –

Hier sass ich nächtlich; hörte vom Mäuerlein
Des Weinbergwegs den wachsenden Laut, den Laut
  Der rings verhohlenen Gewässer
  Neben den Beten der Eingeschlafnen –

Hier kreuzte meinen steigenden Pfad der Weg
Der wilden Dirne, die aus der pfaterosten
  Thalschaft des schwarzen Hochgebirges
  Hölzerne Waare gehäuft zu Markte

Gewaltiges Schritts mir singend vorüber trug,
Friedloses Goldhaar über der Götterstirn
  Sich bändigend, und keusch wie Tiere
  Fahrend in ihrer Pracht des Leibes. –

Hier sprach ich: „Mischleib, Nymphe, Hamadryas –
Nur noch so lang als jetzt Dein beschlagener
  Fusstritt bergab nicht ganz verhallt ist, –
  Als Dir das Ohr in der Luft noch nach hängt, –

Nur noch so lang den Ewigen Schöpfungs Tag
Durch Deine Augen sehn, wie er niederfährt!
  Nur noch so lang durch Deine Nüstern
  Ziehen den Odem die Ersten Nachtwinds!

Dir scheint die Sonne, fruchtet der Regen: Feld
und Herde nährt Dich. Schauder und Kuss verheisst
  Dir die Unendlichkeit des Schoosses;
  Aber wir Anderen sind nicht glückl.“ ‟

can distract from the object he is creating. As a result of this disposition he conceived his poetic activity above all as a contribution to language and the spirit of form. The idea of the affinity between the poetic and the religious vocations which was traceable in Hofmannsthal was given concrete form by Schröder. He renewed the Word for the Christian community in hymns worthy of the traditions of sacred song, in poems in honour of the annual feasts and in simple poetic renderings of the gospels.

Theoretically it may here be objected that poetry is then setting aside its own truth to serve a religious truth, which immediately raises the question of what we really understand by poetic truth. If the carpet of which we spoke at the beginning of this chapter is a curtain separating the inner sanctuary from the body of the faithful, every embellishment on it intimates a truth which can only be revealed to the human understanding by a parable. If there is nothing behind the curtain — no sanctuary and no truth — then the patterns and figures which I read into the carpet enter into an infinite, complementary relationship, to a whole, however, of which I know nothing and which I may equally well call Nothingness as All. Although I can never expect to grasp the substance of this whole in its entirety, yet in searching after it I hope to discover an explanation of my own existence.

P.
VERGILI MARONIS
ECLOGÆ & GEORGICA
LATINE ET GERMANICE
VOLUMEN PRIUS
ECLOGÆ

Virgil's Eclogues, title page

[Handwritten poem in German]

Von Berg zu Berge geht der Gruss,
Die Ferne wird in ihnen zur Nähe:
Wir wollten beid' an seinem Fuss,
Dann trüg's uns langsam in die Höhe.

Hier oben wohnt nun Einsamkeit;
Und doch, ich weiss, du wirst sie segnen.
Die Welt ward gross, der Blick ward weit,
Den soviel tausend heut begegnen.

Was in viel tausend Herzen brennt,
Brennt dann aber auch in meiner Klause;
Fröstelst du!— fühlend ich mich getröstet,
Wir sind im selben Vaterlande.

In certain periods the poet may easily fall a prey to a certain illusion. Finding that the impressions which he receives from without are new, because, for instance, relations between the sexes, means of transport and sources of information have all changed, he believes that he can draw his poetic inspiration directly from reality; he overlooks the fact that since Novalis and Hölderlin poetic testimony has advanced along lines of its own and that to diverge from the point which it has reached amounts to disloyalty towards its truth. The realities of the outside world can only have a stimulating effect on poetry if poetic diction maintains its critical position. The revolutionary impetuosity to which Richard Dehmels' verse owed its immediate effect did not hold good for long. By contrast, the elaborate exuberance and versatile manner of writing of Arno Holz corresponds far more closely to our own view of life even to-day. The ballad, which has occupied its traditional place in our poetry almost without interruption since the eighteenth century and whose form tends to be either purely mythical or else that of didactic allegory, can now only fascinate us in the form of a direct poetic vision or of a demonstrated example.

The incompatibility between the changing influences of the time and the law governing poetic diction can best be studied if we examine the poetic activity of Rainer Maria Rilke in his different phases. In his remarkable essay *Die Sterblichkeit der Musen*, Wladimir Weidlé shrewdly observed that Rilke — and according to Weidlé the same applies to the Russian Alexander Block and the Irishman Yeats — was just as much the creator of his own poetic personality as the creator of his works. That Rilke's fame by far exceeds that of George and Hofmannsthal, Georg Trakl and Oskar Loerke, is certainly partly due to the fact that he succeeds in winning us over in the most subtle manner; everything he has written is significant and is a part of the whole, every letter which is published for posterity partakes of the essence of his poetry and reflects back upon it. Thus here we find the poet's own person once more playing the principal role in the fulfilment of the higher poetic mission. The young poet's assumption of this role is justified when his inner, poetic compulsion allows him to answer honestly in the affirmative the question suggested to him by Rilke: "Must I write?" Hofmannsthal had already stressed the neediness of the poet and defined his position allegorically by comparing him to the saint living as a beggar in a corner under the stairs in his father's house, an unrecognized stranger. However, Hofmannsthal still spoke of the paternal home, thus implying the claim of the unrecognized son to the property of which he was deprived, whereas Rilke's beggar stands at the corner of the road, exposed to every wind of the times. Yet on closer examination we see that for Rilke the poverty of the poet and of poetry is not privation but frugality, the renunciation of all needs. The monk in Rilke's *Stundenbuch*, Saint Francis of Assisi, the deified Buddha, but also the statues in the Louvre, Venice preserved in its ancient splendour, the French cathedrals and the aqueducts of the Roman Campagna are all symbols of this frugality, this self-sufficiency. In their contemplation poetic feeling satisfies its own need; in this lies the signi-

Rilke – the poetic mission again assumed by the poet in person

Rainer Maria Rilke
Etching by L. Albert-Lazard

ficance of their splendid poverty. As long as Rilke remains accessible to the influences of his time, listening to its voices and taking its counsel, he is not fully one with his mission, for there must be no foreign medium between the poet and his poetry. The proximity of God in the Book of Hours, the unrequited love which at the end of the *Aufzeichnungen des Malte Laurids Brigge* appears to the prodigal son as the goal he set out to attain, are allegorical images of the direct relationship of the poet to poetry at which Rilke was aiming. The self-sufficiency of poetry consists in its being a blank space, an empty receptacle, which once filled, however, can transform everything. The poet is the being through which things pass to find their reflection in poetic truth.

We observe how the factor of personal experience has become nothing more than the entrance to the precincts of the poem. In an essay on the works of Johann Sebastian Bach, Oskar Loerke pointed out that the tears which flowed in Bach's Passion music were not his own nor those of anyone else, but arose from

Handwriting of Rainer Maria Rilke

66

the lament which belongs to no-one, though it may dwell in each of us. One could say the same of the 'lament' in Rilke's *Duineser Elegien*. Here the relationship between poet and poem is about to change abruptly. Not only does personal experience become irrelevant by comparison with poetic reality, because it is no more than the impulse which sets off the poem, but it is relegated more and more to the background once it has surrendered its initiating power to the word. This development can be followed with the greatest clarity in the works of Georg Trakl. Certain elements which at first still indicate the presence of a subjective origin appear later on in detached form and fuse with other elements. It would seem as if every step by which the poet advances beyond a certain point carries his verses further up towards untrodden heights. The breathless ascent which in Nietzsche's poetry is that of an experimentalist observing himself, in Trakl's works leads to a concentration of the very language, which becomes rigid under the weight of an unutterable destiny.

In the poems of Oskar Loerke and Georg Trakl the element of personal experience recedes more and more into the background

There is nothing to prevent us from calling Trakl's later poems expressionistic, if this really means anything. Expressionism can only be indirectly defined because in relation to reality it recognizes merely degrees of intensity. When surveying the literary landscape we are struck by the fact that certain features discovered there appear to have a common geological origin, although it is hard to say exactly to what period they belong. *Wanderers Sturmlied* by Goethe was borne of the same subterranean upheaval — inspiring the experiencing ego with ecstasy — as was *Die Silberhütte* by Oskar Loerke. But the language, which in both cases was subject to the same influence, streams forth in Goethe like a hymn whereas in Loerke it is strictly profiled and condensed within itself. When Loerke in one of his poems sums up the chaos of a stormy night in the apparition of a grey moth, the sound of whose whirring wings makes the poet aware of the tension vibrating in his own breast, he has to eliminate from the scene everything which might confine the image by too close a definition. For should he allow this to happen it would interrupt the current which flows through the verses of the poem.

Expressionism only recognizes degrees of intensity

It is significant that Oskar Loerke had a clear idea in advance of how he was going to organize his poetic production. It was to be divided into seven volumes, from which we may assume that when Loerke was jotting down a line or

Oskar Loerke and the extent of poetic production

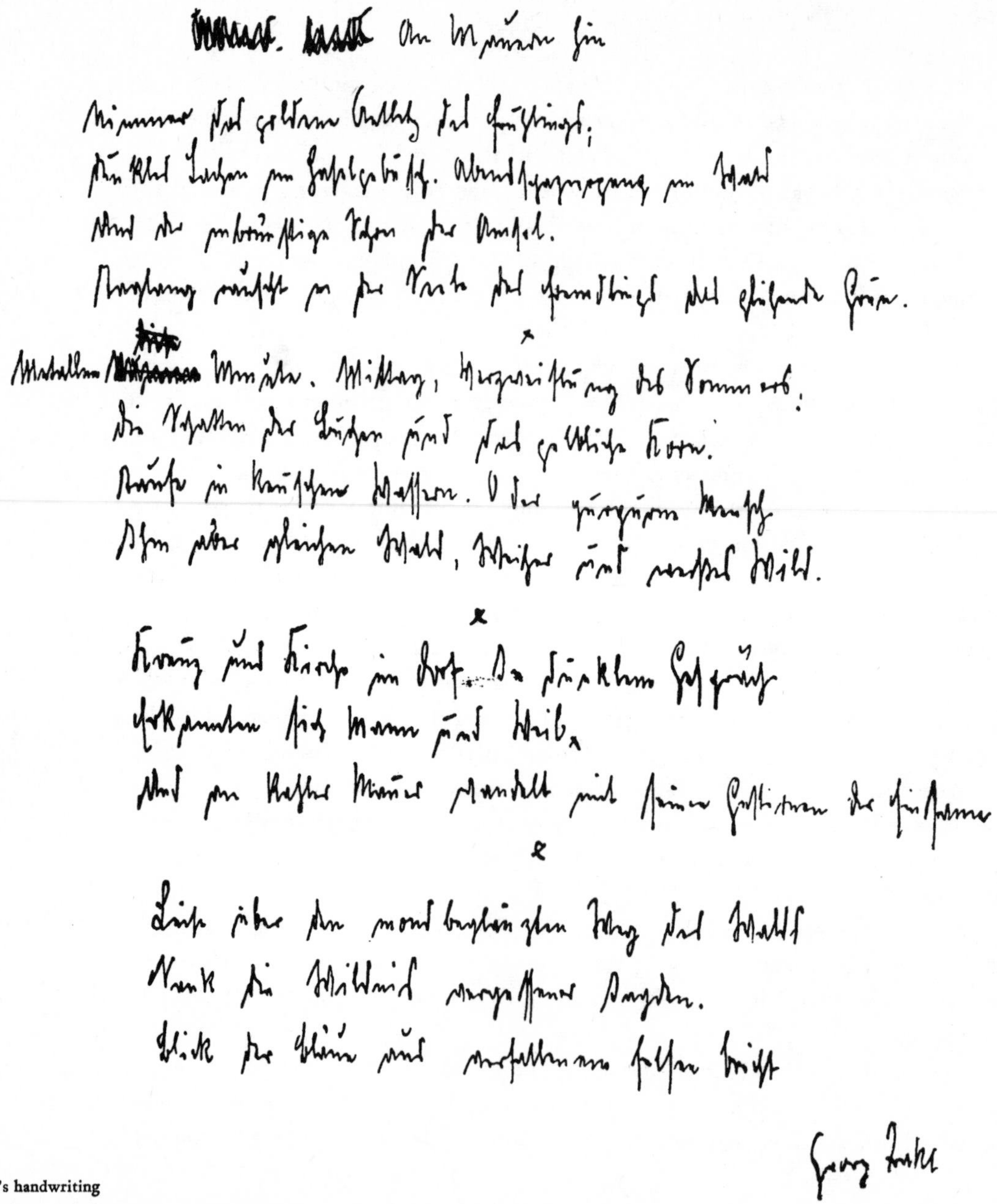

Georg Trakl

Rudolf Borchardt

Theodor Däubler

Walter Benjamin

Ise
asker-Schüler

71
Karl Kraus

Frank Wedekind

Ferdinand Bruckner

Ernst Toller

Georg Kaiser

Heinr
Ma

74
Oskar
Loerke

7
Gottfrie
Ben

polishing up a verse he knew exactly where he intended to place them in the overall plan of his works. Mallarmé also realized at a certain point that apart from a casual poem here and there he must from then on devote himself entirely to the completion of the one all-embracing work whose well-defined plan he had in mind.

To avoid misunderstandings it must be added that this plan of a poet's work is nothing static, but represents the scope which his inspiration demands. In order to appear in its full depth, personal experience requires a more lasting medium, as in one of Loerke's poems the clouds floating past in the evening sky are reflected in the brass of a street-lamp. The lasting nature of the medium reveals the movement in a different manner. This no longer proceeds outside but takes place within the medium, lighting it up with a golden brilliance or filling it with leaden gloom, in short revealing the whole scale of its latent possibilities. The medium of poetry is language, and this may be regarded as the pre-existent order against the background of which the poem presents a moving pattern. Thus the subjective experience appears only as the occasion which allows the poet to grasp the object, the reality of poetic language, just as the street-lamp only provides the occasion which allows the metal to transpose the passing of the clouds into its range of light and shadow.

The expressionist poem has a mediumistic character. It contains neither an 'I' nor a world to which that 'I' refers, but only a neutral 'it'. In fact, expressionist poetry reverts to the mode of expression of myth. Theodor Däubler, in the mighty visions of his different series of poems, is a mythical poet. Else Lasker-Schüler is the ecstatic dancer of her poems. Alfred Mombert gathers round him the cloak of a world-consciousness which only retains the faintest connection with its origin in personal experience.

On the other hand the impersonal language of myth also corresponds to the anonymous voice of the public. Maurice Blanchot, in a very subtle study on the mission of the poet to-day, describes a situation which is evident in the poetry of the period we are considering, when he points out that in former times the current of myth transformed the word into nameless song, whereas to-day we need only step out into the road to plunge into the current of that unceasing, anonymous talk which is the deplorable feature of our public, and that both

The vision as original poetic action in the sense of Novalis

Hebräische Balladen
von
Else Lasker-Schüler

A. R. Meyer Verlag
1   9   1   3
Berlin-Wilmersdorf

Cover designed by Else Lasker-Schüler

The murmur of myth and the noise of the street

currents meet in the consciousness of the poet. In Rilke's *Duineser Elegien* the city is depicted in the empty bustle of a fair. Everything which is displayed and advertised is, in its anonymity and estrangement, the dumb show, as it were, of that myth which only consists of language, its surrounding world having disappeared. The golden statue of the Egyptian god behind the glass door of the museum, round which the street-walkers flit like so many moths, in one of Oskar Loerke's poems, draws a drastic parallel between the unreality of myth and the anonymity of the big city. Yet in the expressionist poetry of the big city we catch a reflection of myth. The city with its constantly changing aspects, the lightning contact which it establishes between the near and the far, but above all because it submerges the individual in a relentlessly proceeding course of events, is the great scene which produces a state of consciousness that would seem to favour a revival of myth. — A fake myth, however, or — if consciousness

78

sees through it — an artificially prepared myth with an ironical turn. The poems of Gottfried Benn swing back and forth like a sensitive pointer between visionary ecstasy and cool statement. Myth is luxury of feeling, which does not imply anything derogatory for it is precisely through this that exuberance and abundance, which cannot be judged on a utilitarian basis, reveal themselves as vital phenomena and lend a wild, exotic splendour to the Bacchanalian procession in which Nietzsche precedes his pupil Benn. Dyonisian. — But can modern consciousness reconcile itself with the irresponsibility of emotions? What is going to happen to the ego, to the experiencing individual pursuing a practical profession, living in a regulated community and relying on empirical knowledge, if the string by which he holds the beautiful kite he has sent up should break?

Oskar Loerke's handwriting

Nur zwei Dinge

Durch so viel Formen geschritten,
durch Ich und Wir und Du,
doch alles blieb erlitten
durch die ewige Frage: wozu?

Das ist eine Kinderfrage.
Dir wurde erst spät bewußt,
es gibt nur eines: ertrage
– ob Sinn, ob Sucht, ob Sage –
dein fernbestimmtes: Du mußt.

Ob Rosen, ob Schnee, ob Meere,
was alles erblühte, verblich,
es gibt nur zwei Dinge: die Leere
und das gezeichnete Ich.

Gottfried Benn.

1953.

Gottfried Benn's handwriting

It is an insurmountable dilemma. It is the great artistic merit of Gottfried Benn that he not only fully recognized this and accepted the splitting of his ego which it imposed, but also succeeded in expressing it very clearly in his poems.

Others have turned their backs on myth and depicted man. Bertolt Brecht draws a critical balance between feelings and circumstances in his poems. The impersonal voice of an announcer, street-singer or crier is used to present the poem, now become anonymous, in objective fashion. Different phases of this development are illustrated by Frank Wedekind, Christian Morgenstern in his Palmström poems and later Klabund and Ringelnatz. Walter Höllerer particularly stressed this aspect and commented upon it in his anthology of modern poetry, under the heading *Transit*. In his collections of satirical poems, *(Herz auf Taille*, etc.). Erich Kästner pitilessly exposes the estranged double of his ego. He splits it up into its components, unmasks its feelings and dissects its moral complexes. As a humorist, however, he sees nothing strange in the fact that his own person remains invisible and is reflected as a caricature. This is why — however caustic and to the point his cynical wit may be — we can always trace in Kästner's poems a shame-faced or resigned benevolence towards the curious species of man.

Myth abandoned in favour of the portrayal of man

'Söhne' by Gottfried Benn
Cover-design by Ludwig Meidner

The spectrum of the novel

Virginia Woolf on the novel

In her very intelligent and illuminating essay *Phases of Fiction* Virginia Woolf writes the following, from her own professional experience: "For some reason not here to be examined, fiction is the most hospitable of hosts; fiction to-day draws to itself writers who would even yesterday have been poets, dramatists, pamphleteers, historians. The 'novel' as we still call it with such parsimony of language, is clearly splitting apart into books which have nothing in common but this one inadequate title."

Every novel – often even by the same author – is different

Even a superficial glance at the German novels of the first half of the century is enough to confirm this observation. To complicate the matter still further, it is impossible to overlook the fact that some authors who introduce a revolutionary style on the stage write their narrative works in a classical manner, as, for instance, Gerhard Hauptmann who in his brilliant, early work *Die Weber* presented his audience with a picture of actual social conditions, whereas his novel *Der Narr in Christo Emanuel Quint* is written in almost patriarchal style and *Die Insel der Grossen Mutter* is reminiscent of the moralistic phantasies of the eighteenth century.

It may also happen that the novels of one and the same author are so completely different from one another that each would seem to be written according to its own special formula. Alfred Döblin's *Berlin Alexanderplatz*, if we consider the characters and events portrayed, is a modern picaresque story, whereas *Babylonische Wandrung* — the book which immediately followed it — is a burlesque which in the luxuriant flora of its language is more reminiscent of the story of the giants Gargantua and Pantagruel than of the escapades of a poor rascal who has to live by his wits. The trilogy *Die Schlafwandler* by Hermann Broch differs from volume to volume not only in style but also in the form. Later on, in exile, under the influence of the impressions he had retained from

Gerhart Hauptmann
Drawing by Emil Orlik (1924)

82

the time spent under arrest, awaiting death at the hands of the Gestapo, Broch produced the astonishing linguistic creation *Der Tod des Vergil,* which presents not a single feature which could lead one to suspect that it was written by the same author as *Die Schlafwandler.* In the works of Thomas Mann and Hermann Hesse the variations of style are not quite so marked. Yet what a difference there is between *Die Buddenbrooks* and *Die Geschichten Jaakobs!* And although the two works were written at such a close interval, what a contrast between the meditative prose of Hesse's Indian parable *Siddharta* and the vehement *staccato* of the Swiss tale *Klingsor's letzter Sommer!* Since the novel may take such different forms in the hands of a single author, it is not surprising that many different authors stretch the meaning of the term novel, as representing a particular literary species, to the utmost. An attempt has been made to escape from the predicament by reintroducing the discarded term "epic" — since genuine epics are no longer written — with a different meaning. There is, however, a disadvantage in this from the point of view of literary criticism. If we honour a poet by designating his work as an epic it is always intended as praise. The possibility that an epic poet might not necessarily be a great poet is simply not considered. The French have found a way out by using the expression *roman-fleuve,* which is quite appropriate inasmuch as such broad rivers of prose fiction very often end in a delta in which all that is left of the original, strong current is dissipated in separate channels.

The tradition of historical fiction has continued unbroken ever since the romantic period in both England and Germany. However, due to the new vital consciousness which was gaining ground at the turn of the century and which made historical reality directly dependent on historical experience and intuitive perception of historical events, irrational forces began to figure as the active agents serving to unify the multiplicity of historical phenomena. Ina Seidel's novels *Das Wunschkind* and *Lennacker,* in spite of their accuracy of historical detail, have a visionary source and relate to mythical ideas. The unyielding optimism with which the poetess Ricarda Huch, as the spiritual leader of the women's movement of her generation, carried forward her ideal of liberty like a banner, was so great that it enabled her to reconcile on an ideal plane the conflicting forces of man's daemonic nature and his reason. It is no accident that

Cover of first edition, by K. E. Mende

The epic novel and the 'roman fleuve'

*The historical novel
Ina Seidel, Ricarda Huch,
Gertrud von Le Fort*

Ricarda Huch
Aus Der Triumphgasse
Lebensskizzen
Verlegt bei Eugen Diederichs in Jena 1924

Drawing by Wilhelm Heise

she drew her happiest inspiration from the period of the Italian *Risorgimento*, for the classical Italian feeling for form immediately captures revolutionary tendencies and perpetuates them in an ideal pose.

Ricarda Huch was of an extremely lyrical temperament. The same is true of Ina Seidel and also the Catholic authoress Gertrud von le Fort *(Das Schweisstuch der Veronika* and *Der Papst aus dem Ghetto)*. The lyrical impulse remains perceptible in their prose works and gives their novels poetic form. These are poetic in the complete cycle which they portray and in the balanced distribution of their component elements. In Ina Seidel's *Wunschkind* the northern and the southern part of the empire, as formative spirit and receptive imagination, assume the mutually complementary relationship of two opposite poles, as do the statesman Cavour and the visionary Garibaldi in Ricarda Huch's *Der Kampf um Rom.*

Ricarda Huch's handwriting
From 'Aus der Triumphgasse'

84

When we speak of the introduction of poetic features into the historical novel, what we mean is the use of symbolic figures in the composition of the historical picture. In this connection we may cite Werner Bergengruen's *Am Himmel wie auf Erden* and the Prussian historical novel *Der Vater* by Jochen Klepper.

A danger inherent in cyclic form is that the straightforward tendency may be diverted into esoteric channels. Hermann Broch was aware of this danger when he was wondering how he should end his novel *Der Tod des Vergil*. The great dialogue between the dying poet and the Roman Emperor Augustus on the subject of the Aenead — Virgil wishes the poem to be destroyed at his death, while Augustus wishes to preserve it in the interest of the State — makes the completion of the work a matter of debate and touches on Broch's dilemma with regard to his own work.

The cyclic tendency and its dangers

Broch: 'Der Tod des Vergil'

In another great novel of that period, the epilogue of which makes a provisional impression, *Fluss ohne Ufer* by Hans Henny Jahnn, the conflict between mind and nature is portrayed in a plot which has no end. When man's primitive instinct takes the upper hand, the mind has to accept the role of an isolated and constantly endangered outsider and wait for an opportunity which will allow it to harness the blind energy of the instinctive force in its own service. Sometimes the mind is dependent on the flesh and requires its assistance to achieve its own purposes. The friendship which links the composer Gustav Anias Horn and the sailor Tutein, their Odyssey of many adventures on gruesome shores and their descent into the underworld of nature are the theme of the novel, which comes to no end even with their death. In just the same way, the mental adventure on which Musil's hero Ulrich embarks has no recognizable goal. He is seeking that primary state of reality to which we have direct access in moments of intuition, when we are detached from all interest in the world and the mind is not pursuing any particular idea. But how can one seek what one already possesses? How can one grasp what is intrinsically impalpable? How approach in words what is wordless in experience? The only possible procedure is to try by means of differentiation to define this other state of reality ever more closely, starting by critical examination of those qualities which man attributes to himself as a matter of course and consideration of the possibility that if there is "another state" of reality, then may there not also be 'another state' of man?

Hans Henny Jahnn: 'Fluss ohne Ufer'

Musil: 'Der Mann ohne Eigenschaften', or the search for the other state

Closer analysis of Musil's novel reveals a principle of form which may be called 'broken unity'. We have already encountered this principle in the poems of Oskar Loerke and, still more clearly evident, in those of Gottfried Benn. The dramatic works of Georg Kaiser, which are classical but at the same time expressive, would also appear to conform to this principle.

Virginia Woolf is expressing a similar thought when she writes in the essay quoted at the beginning of this chapter that we demand of the novel a synthesis, and mentions the two tendencies which should be synthesized: "The novel . . . can follow life; it can amass details. But can it also select? Can it symbolize? Can it give us an epitome as well as an inventory?" The answer would be that this depends on the circumstances, that is to say on whether there is any principle of order present which subtly transforms the rectilinear progress of the novel into a curve. To put it more clearly: without Dublin and what it symbolized for Joyce it would have been hard to give *Ulysses* a cyclic structure.

Without the background of Venice, Henry James would have found it very difficult to illustrate in figurative language the gradual dissolution of the vital force on approaching the invisible boundary of death, in his novel *The Wings of the Dove*. If Proust had not been so deeply rooted in the civilization of France he might have succeeded in recapturing the past in moments of personal experience, but he could never have recaptured it in all the fullness in which it was revealed to him by the façade of Amiens Cathedral, like a bible carved in stone. The curious contradiction in which Musil stands to the subject of his novel *Der Mann ohne Eigenschaften* is really due to the fact that Ulrich, although he plans to make an expedition into the unexplored realm of the 'other state', actually never sets foot beyond the frontiers of the Habsburg empire — the 'Kakania' of which Musil so affectionately makes fun — and remains, like Tann-

häuser, a captive in the Venusberg of his own personal culture. This is the only reason why it strikes us as strange that in notes referring to his novel Musil calls his hero a man of fighting instincts or a man of action. Ulrich's activity is actually limited to cutting like a straight line through the concentric circles which bear witness to the egocentric character of all culture. We may assume that Musil was quite aware of the irony in the paradoxical circumstance that the 'other state' which Ulrich is pursuing is also a circle, although one that has been purged of every peculiarity. It is the fiction of a world without any definable content, a universe which engulfs every motion of the mind. If we pursue the imperial conception of 'Kakania' to its ultimate spiritual sublimation we arrive at something similar to that which Musil calls the 'other state' of reality. Thus there is no necessity for Ulrich to set out anywhere in order to seek this other state, just as he is not compelled by his love for his sister Agatha, which she whole-heartedly returns, to undertake any dangerous adventure because he already possesses what he desires. It is therefore only a question of refining and sublimating an idea.

The paradoxical nature of a search for an object already possessed, undertaken for the purpose of justification, is also a dominant note in the novels and stories of Frank Kafka. Musil treats the paradox ironically; Kafka sees the paradoxical nature of human existence reflected in it. When reading Kafka one has the impression that it is not the other, that is, the primary state of reality which has to be rediscovered, as in Musil, but that, on the contrary, we are compelled to live in that other state and are searching in vain for the explainable or justifiable state of the world that we have lost. Musil attempts to register the dividing line which separates what was formerly one complete world into two disparate halves as accurately as possible and to form an opinion of its distinctive quality. Kafka sees in the rupture the basic condition of human existence and tracks down the open wound in every phase of life.

Franz Kafka: the incomprehensible state of the world

Drawings by Franz Kafka

87

Page from Franz Kafka's manuscript:
'Der Prozess'

abends, Am Vorabend seines 31 Geburtstages – es war gegen 9 Uhr
die Zeit der Stille auf den Strassen – kamen zwei
Herren in K. Wohnung in Gehröcken, bleich und fett,
mit scheinbar unverrückbaren Cylinderhüten. Nach
einer kleinen Förmlichkeit bei der Wohnungstür wegen
des ersten Eintretens wiederholte sich die gleiche
Förmlichkeit in grösserem Umfange vor K's. Tür. Ohne
dass ihm der Besuch angekündigt gewesen wäre, sass
K. gleichfalls schwarz angezogen in einem Sessel
in der Nähe der Türe und zog langsam
neue scharf sich über die Finger spannende Hand-
schuhe an, in der Haltung wie man Gäste erwartet.

Musil: the Utopian state of the world

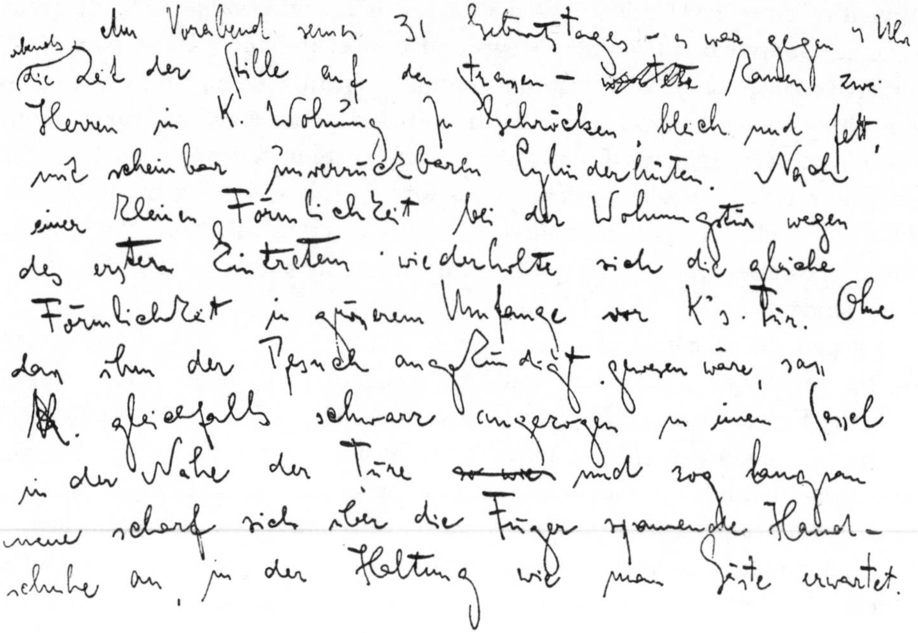

Here time becomes short, whereas with Musil, as is appropriate to the Utopian character of his novel, time would appear to have no end. The fragmentary nature of Kafka's novels and stories is direct evidence of the rupture which is both his point of departure and the point towards which he sees everything converge; correspondingly, in Musil's novel, the indefinitely postponed adventure expresses the asymptotic approach to the infinitely elusive goal.

The former imperial conception appears more tangibly in the novels of Joseph Roth *(Radetzkymarsch* and *Die Kapuzinergruft),* in *Die Standarte* by Alexander Lernet-Holenia and – after the war – in *Die Strudlhofstiege* by Heimito von Doderer. We shall revert to this later.

The rule of variation and repetition found in Thomas Mann's works

At this point it becomes clear that the seven years which Thomas Mann's hero Hans Castorp spends far away from his Hanseatic home, on the 'magic mountain' of Davos, and the current problems which occupy his mind during his rest-cures, are connected with the ruptured relationship between progressive action and poetic totality. The rule which is followed produces a somewhat desultory effect. The strictly chronological course of events is abandoned and instead we have something more resembling a spiral, which varies, repeats and probes more deeply into certain themes as it advances. This principle was clearly explained by Thomas Mann in his Joseph tetralogy. There is, however, another point which he did not mention there. *'Zauberberg' and 'Joseph-Romane'*

The question occupying Mann in these novels — in contrast to the *Zauberberg* — was the process of development and periodic recurrence of mythical forms and conceptions. Since the poet alone — and solely through language — is the percipient and guardian of these legitimate elements, the question arises, as in the sphere of poetry, whether we are here dealing merely with an intellectual game or with a genuine, higher or deeper form of experience. The author of the Joseph tetralogy refuses to give up his ironical, impartial standpoint and is quite prepared on one occasion to perceive a higher meaning in that which another time he may regard as merely a well-contrived figure of speech. For this reason it does not surprise us to learn that it was almost a shock to Thomas Mann when he realized, having come upon Hesse's *Glasperlenspiel* while he was pondering the subject of *Doktor Faustus*, his affinity to Hesse's poetry. The fact that in both cases the plot is dominated by a musical theme does not even appear to me as the decisive factor, especially since with Thomas Mann it is the problems surrounding genius which form the background of the musical symbol, whereas with Hesse it is the problems surrounding civilization. What I consider decisive is the ironic deflection which becomes apparent in both cases in the poetic symbol which we are asked to accept, although it is proved to be of an artificial nature. That Thomas Mann, as I said before, was prepared on one occasion to perceive a higher meaning in something which on another he would regard as a well-contrived figure of speech, is confirmed by the fact that his game of beads is celebrated as an act of worship while being the product of deliberate action and deep meditation. *'Doktor Faustus' and 'Glasperlenspiel'*

Considering the matter more profoundly we may say that both cases represent extreme examples of the German novel of character. We have defined education as participation in the world. This definition corresponds to the view held by Max Scheler, who differentiates between three types of knowledge: the know- *Sublimation of the character novel The limits of education*

HERMANN HESSE

SUHRKAMP

Cover designed by Günter Böhmer

The zone of adventure

Ernst Jünger

ledge of achievement or control, such as natural sciences and technology impart; the knowledge of genuine education which ensures man's participation in the world, and religious knowledge which is the knowledge of things beyond this world. It is obvious that it is going to be very difficult in the long run to hold the borderline between the knowledge of achievement and the knowledge of education, unless we transform it, as Hesse does, into a preclusive frontier and reserve a special domain, a pedagogic province as 'Kastalia' is referred to — significantly recalling Goethe — for the cultivation of knowledge useful to life. However, since this precaution involves renouncing verification against reality, the relationship between the cultural and the religious phases of education begins to waver. Pure mind is obviously not of this world, but does this mean in the same sense as the divine is not of this world? Does culture contribute to the understanding of other-wordly things or does it not really replace it? It would seem as if Hesse, in order to avoid this dilemma, finally abandoned the symbol of the game of glass beads and linked education to reality and achievement once more.

To a certain extent this is also applicable to Thomas Mann, if one compares the artful simplicity of his Felix Krull with the symbolic ambiguity of his young Joseph.

Between the hermetically closed sphere of a province like 'Kastalia' or a refuge like the 'magic mountain' and the domain of technology there exists an intermediate zone which remains in touch with both. This is the zone of adventure. Here we find the writer pursuing his own adventurous way, with the symbolic world stretching like a chain of mountains along the horizon on one side and on the other the workshop world of technology. The landscape is that which Ernst Jünger described in his story *Auf den Marmorklippen,* but which had already been outlined in his novel *Afrikanische Spiele.* The essay is adventure in literary form. And since the mind is adventurous by nature, the essayist Musil often goes so far that the novel-writer Musil cannot keep up with him. The same thing happens in the case of Ernst Jünger, whose perceptive talent constantly amazes us, but only, however, as long as he hunts his prey on open ground and captures it in strikingly apt language in diaries or essays, but not when he presents it carefully arranged within the framework of a story.

The novel of adventure is the phase which precedes the character novel; it appeals to the author whenever the notion of education begins to be challenged. The adventurer is a key figure in the novels of Rudolf Borchardt. Max Dauthendey, who longed for distant horizons and having reached them longed for home, and who still wrote genuine *Lieder,* suggested exotic vitality in his novel *Raubmenschen.* The favourite heroes of Alexander Lernet-Holenia are also adventurers, the most exalted of them being Prince Eugene of Savoy. Werner Helwig is another writer who loves adventure.

One part of the adventurer's role is constantly to provoke the ordered system from which he has broken away and expose its hypocrisy and hollowness. There is food for thought in the fact that in post-war literature the provocative element has been exploited to the extreme and no other figure has approached the popularity of the adventurer. The adventurer who exploits the shakiness of a decaying social structure is a swindler in the same sense as Casanova in the eighteenth century and, in contemporary literature, Felix Krull and the hero of Robert Neumann's tale of a swindler.

In Thomas Mann's *Memoiren des Hochstaplers Felix Krull* the character novel is a humorous foil for the novel of adventure. In other words, the society novel, which is found relatively seldom in German literature, is here replaced by two mirrors between which the image of the hero is ironically reflected back and forth. The memoirs reveal what Krull thinks of himself; his adventures show what he really is; the medium in which the two perspectives meet is European society at the beginning of the century.

Swindlers

In this connection we may note that the country which gave us the genuine society novel is that which had been forced by the two powers Germany and France into the role of the adventurer: Alsace. Christoph von Grimmelshausen, the author of *Simplicius Simplicissimus,* was an Alsatian. The adventurous and tragic part played by this strongly individual country, which should have been a mediator but became an apple of discord, was portrayed in an effective and vivid manner by René Schikele in his novel in three volumes: *Das Erbe am Rhein.* Otto Flake was another to establish a link between Alsace and Europe.

Alsace between humanity and civilization

Heinrich Mann also contended with the dialectics of love between different countries. Whereas Schikele, however, was used to living in two languages since

Heinrich Mann and the patriotic dilemma

Cover designed by Siegfried Oelke (1959)

Voltaire and Zola as champions of social justice

childhood, so that he could cross the frontier in both directions on the flying carpet of association, Heinrich Mann was the oppositional champion of an ideal which continually exposed the seamy side and the failings of the civilization into which he was born. The ardour and greatness of the Renaissance were as foreign to the Imperial age as was the genuine concord of a civilization to the Weimar republic. The grotesque figure of Professor Unrat, who is compelled to feel ashamed of his secret dreams of reckless passion while standing at his desk in public, is just as characteristic of this incompatibility as is the shame felt by the young crown prince in the later, unfinished work *Traurige Geschichte von Friedrich dem Grossen*, over his father's scorn and reprimands because of his admiration for Voltaire and the tragic tirade. The same element of social criticism which strikes us in the works of Zola, Maupassant and Anatole France is unmistakably present in satires like *Der Untertan* and the biting mockery of the satiated middle class in *Schlaraffenland*. In Heinrich Mann, however, it is more aggressive, more damaging. For in Germany the protective layer of social reservations is on one hand more solid and hence impermeable to criticism, while on the other — and this applies particularly to the intellectuals — it is non-existent. Too little attention is generally paid to this point. As the German intellectual is only interested in possessing social status as a matter of form, he is always prepared to regard social criticism as criticism of every form of society, whereas in France even writers with extreme views react to drastic criticism with a certain reserve. The complete rejection of every social tie involves the complete depreciation of whole periods, while on the other hand it strengthens the prejudices held with respect to them. It was under the weight of this dual distortion that the Weimar republic broke down in the 'thirties. Up to now, scarcely any positive grounds could be determined for assuming that we shall be spared further tests of this nature in the future.

At all events, the basic feeling expressed in Heinrich Mann's works was an ardent and suffering patriotism. He felt it was a fault in our civilization that there existed in Germany no platform such as that from which Zola delivered his *J'accuse*. This represented a betrayal of the individual who is great enough to stand up against the society of his time, justifying his action in the name of 'culture', and is acclaimed by a later generation. Voltaire's voice was heard

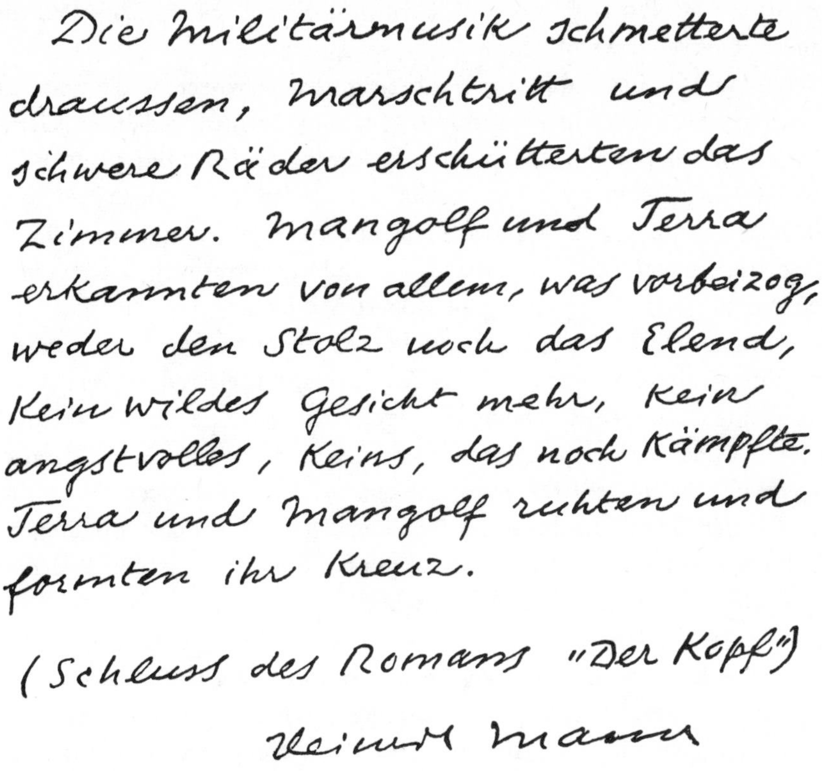

Die Militärmusik schmetterte draussen, marschtritt und schwere Räder erschütterten das Zimmer. Mangolf und Terra erkannten von allem, was vorbeizog, weder den Stolz noch das Elend, kein wildes Gesicht mehr, kein angstvolles, keins, das noch kämpfte. Terra und Mangolf ruhten und formten ihr Kreuz.

(Schluss des Romans „Der Kopf")

Heinrich Mann

Handwriting of Heinrich Mann

calling for investigation of the Calas case. Zola's accusation contributed to assure that justice was done in the case of Captain Dreyfus. If the world of culture, whose richness and 'depth' in contrast to mere civilization had been so loudly proclaimed in the 'twenties, could fail at the decisive moment, then in Heinrich Mann's eyes the derided civilization was preferable.

Döblin, whose exclusive preference for the great solitary figures: Dostojewski, Strindberg, Knut Hamsun, gradually gave way to a grudging partiality for the more sociable literature of France and the Latin style, learnt to appreciate the advantages of civilization as an emigrant. Other writers also underwent this change of interest from the individual to the social sphere, above all the essayist and critic Walter Benjamin.

Otto Julius Bierbaum
Caricature by O. Gulbransson

It would be both unjust and short-sighted to expect of German literature a type of novel for which its tradition has never prepared it. In Germany, the society novel presents the picture of one particular *milieu*, not of European society in general. Fontane's Berlin novels deal with society in the Prussian borderlands. Thomas Mann's Buddenbrooks are Hanseatics. The family in Schikele's novel *Das Erbe am Rhein* and the Strasburg society he describes belong to Alsace. The setting of Robert Musil's novel is Viennese society. The Bohemian, artistic circles portrayed in their unconventional, free-and-easy aspect by Otto Julius Bierbaum in *Prinz Kuckuck* and their refined relatives described by Isolde Kurz in her *Vanadis* also have a character peculiar to themselves.

The association of narrative literature with a certain town or landscape is, in Germany, an inherent feature of the species. The great success recently obtained by Günter Grass with his novel *Die Blechtrommel* is, in my opinion, due among other things to the fact that the scene of the first part is unmistakably Danzig, and later on Gerresheim near Düsseldorf.

A widespread, preconceived opinion exists to the effect that the qualities Hesse reveals in his *Steppenwolf* are greater than those revealed in the stories he wrote before the first crisis in his life, the setting of which is generally his native Swabia. It will be generally admitted that Hesse was compelled by artistic necessity to go beyond these early stories. It is questionable, however, whether we are justified in taking his private crisis or the crisis of the times as a criterion of value. Present-day literature appears to be rediscovering old-established truths. Born

Local or universal?

story-tellers like the Swiss Otto F. Walter and Jürg Federspiel and the Austrians Herbert Eisenreich and Hans Lebert base their narratives on the reality of the world around them. Adepts of this poetic realism can be found among the authors of narrative literature in the first half of the century right up to our own time.

The small world

It would be mistaken to assume, however, that this thesis implies that the aim pursued is the portrayal of a certain *milieu*, or the achievement of local colour, or the like. This is why I have constantly emphasized the German's striving after education, which leads him to pursue an innate conception of something beyond the horizon of life in which the individual, eluding society, may hope to find his own fulfilment. This is certainly also the origin of the German's partiality for the odd character, the outsider or the eccentric, which incidentally had such a lasting effect on the foreigner's conception of the typical German that after 1870 it came as a painful surprise to many to discover the new type of economic or military strategist. E. T. A. Hoffmann's band-master Kreisler, the soulful, gentle musician Schmucke in Balzac's *Cousin Pons* and also Heinrich Heines clumsy boy with the wooden sword were imaginary characters displaying the strangest mixture of vague reverie, simplicity of mind and sentimentality. The admirable Madame de Staël also contributed to this impression by her description of the country of poets and thinkers.

Eccentrics

If we take a look at our literature we cannot really say that this impression is wrong. Are not Quintus Fixlein, the little schoolmaster Maria Wutz and other of Jean Paul's oddities each something like a miniature edition of some orignal genius? Is E. T. A. Hoffmann's punch-bowl not a sturdier version of the witches' kitchen in Goethe's *Faust?* Are not Georg Büchner's *Lenz*, Heinrich von Kleist's *Michael Kohlhaas* and Eduard Mörike's *Maler Nolten* obstinate outsiders? Wilhelm Raabe also added a number of portraits to this collection. There was something morose about many of these figures, which resulted from the atmosphere of the small state and the narrowness of the provincial town. In Grillparzer's *Der arme Spielmann* the hero is an unrecognized genius, like Balzac's Frenhofer; Immermann's *Münchhausen* is a genius gone to the bad. And touching on the tragic element in the German character inevitably brings to mind the figure of *Peter Schlemihl,* who sold his own shadow.

In stressing this particular factor in the German story-teller's art we are therefore not referring to any provincial eccentricity but to a physiognomical peculiarity.

German literature is like a map revealing the geographical diversity of the country, and a traveller therein can become acquainted with many different towns and landscapes. Ludwig Thoma is the great poet of his native Bavaria. The Silesian Hermann Stehr is superior to Gerhart Hauptmann as a prose writer. The Swabian Emil Strauss had a poetic talent which was sound and self-willed, if not of great scope. Carl Zuckmayer's poetic personality is inseparably linked to his native Rhineland-Hesse. *Der fröhliche Weinberg, Katharina*

The map of German literature

Carl Zuckmayer

95

thendey, who longed for distant lands when he was at home and died of home-sickness when he had reached them, came from Würzburg. Another native of Würzburg was Leonhard Frank, who told his life-story in *Links wo das Herz ist*. Having started as a painters' apprentice he then moved to Munich in order to study art. Then, as so often happens with young talents, life in Bohemian society revealed his real gift. His first novel, *Die Räuberbande*, described all sorts of youthful escapades in his native town. The success he achieved with this led him to continue writing. The small towns along the river Main, with the astute, self-willed Franconian race which inhabits them, are the background of his narrative works. Although seemingly realistic, the source of Frank's inspiration is visionary. Only he is not satisfied with taking the images as they appear to him, but in putting them into words adapts them and condenses them into a few significant traits. In the same way as he realistically adapts what he has perceived with the inward eye, he also often transforms his melancholy ponderings into sound and practical coin, so that he is often considered as a didactic writer, which would, however, be in absolute contradiction to his stubborn individualism. The story *Karl und Anna* and the novel *Bruder und Schwester* in fact reveal an unshakable confidence in intuitive knowledge such as is only to be found in the same degree in Kleist. Frank also had to leave his country during the Third Reich. He had been living in Berlin since the 'twenties. He escaped to France and then to the United States. After the war he was one of the first to return. In Würzburg he faced the ruins of the world of his youth. The spiritual unity, too, in which he had believed with the optimism of the born practician, was split.

The expressionistic trait in Frank's works is perhaps more striking to-day than it was thirty years ago. We have already stated that expressionism is a phenomenon which cannot be dated, but consists in a certain degree of intensity in the language used. The rediscovery of the baroque period, which occurred about the same time as the appearance of expressionism, was connected with an increased receptivity for expressive images which are not dependent on logical concatenation but are directly perceived by our consciousness. The inner life of the spirit is moved — the conception is a residuum. If certain expressive forms

Leonhard Frank, the stubborn German

LEONHARD FRANK
DIE MUTTER
MIT 9 HOLZSCHNITTEN VON
FRANS MASEREEL

Expressionist masters

96

Woodcut by E. L. Kirchner (1924)

Johannes Urzidil

are to regain their former fascination, then the vital consciousness of the percipient must be raised to the same pitch as that of the artist who carved such forms in stone or sent his metaphors soaring beyond the horizon of the everyday world. The baroque style is irreconcilable with classicism. The former is studied, yet its aim is not to drape the artistic theme but to present the work in an original fashion. The expressionist's resentment at the stylized author — such as Georg Heym secretly felt for Stefan George — arises from the fact that he refuses under any circumstances to concede as ornament to the person of the author that which has its rightful place only in the objective order of the work. This dissension is still alive to-day and its fundamental cause is not always recognized. Thus the younger generation of writers detests the alleged or conscious stylization of the person and ardently advocates a radically purified form or structure. It rejects Ernst Jünger and commends Gottfried Benn.

The talent for independent and heightened forms of expression is more developed in certain countries and towns than elsewhere. Prague has its own expressionism, revealed in the novels of Johannes Urzidil *(Die verlorene Geliebte, Prager Tryptichon, Das grosse Halleluja)*. Interest in the possibilities of language and the individuality of words is a feature of this trend. Aware of the teeming diversity of linguistic forms hidden beneath the surface on which our conscious speech traces its modest lines — an inexhaustible fund of instruments with which to satisfy our urge for expression — the poet plunges like a diver into the deep, in search of treasure. What he brings up are stories, legends, folk-tales, dreams, which once released from the trammels of an imposed, rational meaning are restored in full to their original freshness. The meaning of a story differs depending on whether one asks: What meaning does this story have for me? — Or: What does this story express in itself? The autonomous expressive value of Franz Kafka's prose has been pointed out in a publication by Max Bense. Unfortunately he made a 'theory' of his discovery. Oskar Loerke presents the matter in the right light when he refers to Johann Sebastian Bach's, Herder's and Jean Paul's domain of artistic production as their 'invisible realm'. For the poet, critic, interpreter and dramatist Karl Kraus, publisher of the periodical *Die Fackel*, in which almost all of the articles were contributed by himself, language is the invisible realm. Kafka also transfers us to an invisible realm in which we have to search for meanings, whereas the wordless qualities are alarmingly obtrusive. If we take this feeling of a wordless presence, which in the first place is expression and is nearly always distorted by conceptual language, as heuristic principle, we find other, similar literary phenomena. The short stories of Georg Britting, the setting of which is the flat country around Regensburg, along the edge of the Danube, are not based on anything that can be expressed in words but on a speechless impulse which finds its expression in changes of appearance or colour, in magic signs and deep-ringing tones and sometimes even in words. The invisible realm into which we are led by Britting is populated by huntsmen, fishermen and peasants, whose taciturnity is due to the fact that they communicate with the other world in which man is but an ephemeral presence by the language of signs, which preceded the language of words and will perhaps succeed it again in the fullness of time. For the word was born of stillness and will return to stillness.

Drawing by R. Schlichter

An der Donau

Der Damm ist schilfentblösst und blumenleer.
Spuren im Schlamm, zickzack, verstört, und hin und her,
Wie hundgehetzt,
Im Kreis gestolpert und zuletzt
Im Sumpf versunken und Morast.
Schief aus dem Schlamm, verkrallt und sturmzerfetzt,
Ein krummer Weidenast.

Georg Britting

Handwriting of Georg Britting

The poetic spell woven by
Ernst Penzoldt

Ernst Penzoldt, self-portrait

The poet as healer:
Hans Carossa

The Franconian Ernst Penzoldt, a native of Erlangen, possesses the enchanting gift of the real story-teller, who never takes the world for granted as something already familiar, for it is precisely the most important thing which is often overlooked. So much is just waiting for the poet to reveal. Like Jean Paul, whom he resembles in his humour, Penzoldt retains in face of the world the faculty of wonder found in a child, whose artless comments on what it sees are like a mirror held before the grown-up world, in which many see themselves as fools. It is the innocence of genius which he loves most; his favourite heroes are *Der arme Chatterton*, the beautiful boy *Idolino* and *Squirrel* who is fortune's child. Like all humorists he believes in an ideal of human purity, beauty and greatness of which he only finds a distorted reflection in the curved mirror of reality. The young King Sebastian of Portugal in the play *Die Portugalesische Schlacht*, who is killed while fighting the Moors in Africa and in whose death his people refuses to believe, is an ideal figure so far superior to reality that he exacts the right to return to earth once more in the form of a double — the false Sebastian. Here again the vision which gives the lie to outward appearances proves itself to be the primary reality.

Hans Carossa remained loyal to the Bavarian and Austrian border-country round Passau all his life; his best books reflect memories of his youth and early years as a doctor in that neighbourhood. He was an observer who gathered his main impressions through the eye. Although he aimed at a classical purity of expression his fundamental attitude was romantic, which may explain why his style becomes rather colourless when he attempts to move beyond the sphere of his immediate experience. During the war, while tending the wounded on the Roumanian front, he had occasion to observe human suffering and saw in it the mute expression of nature, fate and human existence. The anonymous character of suffering, which ever and again leads a doctor to the brink of an abyss, the depths of which he cannot sound with all the means at his command,

Stefan Andres

Hermann Kasack

René Schickele

Ernst Penzoldt

Luise Rinser

Elisabeth Langgässer

Gertrud von Le Fort

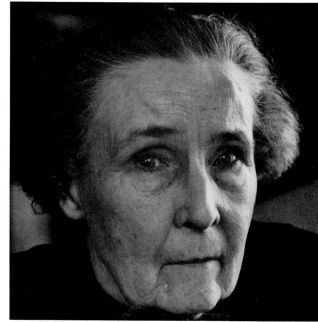

Ina Seidel

Ricard
Hu

104
Carl
Zuckmayer

10
Leonhar
Frar

Georg von der Vring

Karl Krolow

Georg Britting

Wilhelm Lehmann

Wern
Bergengru

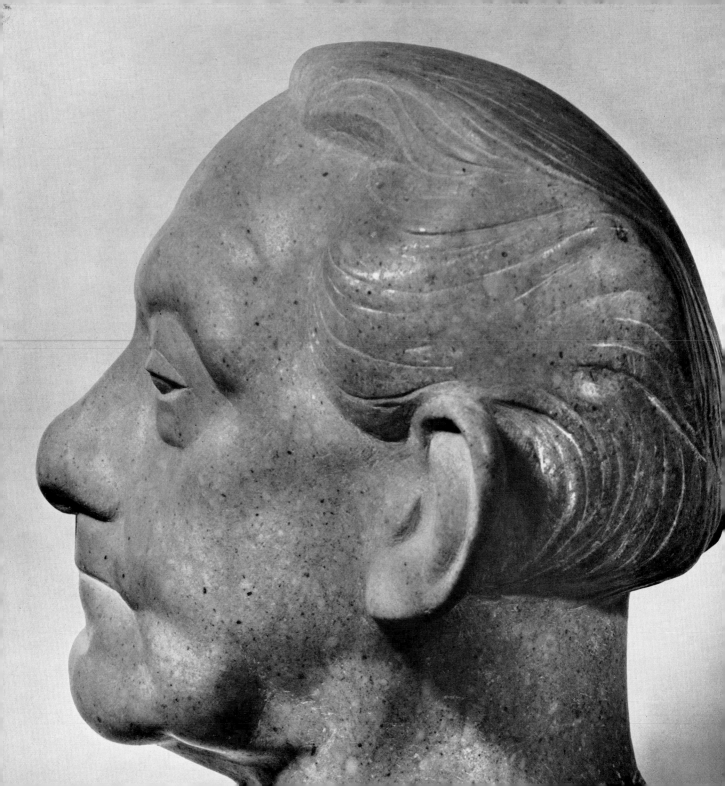

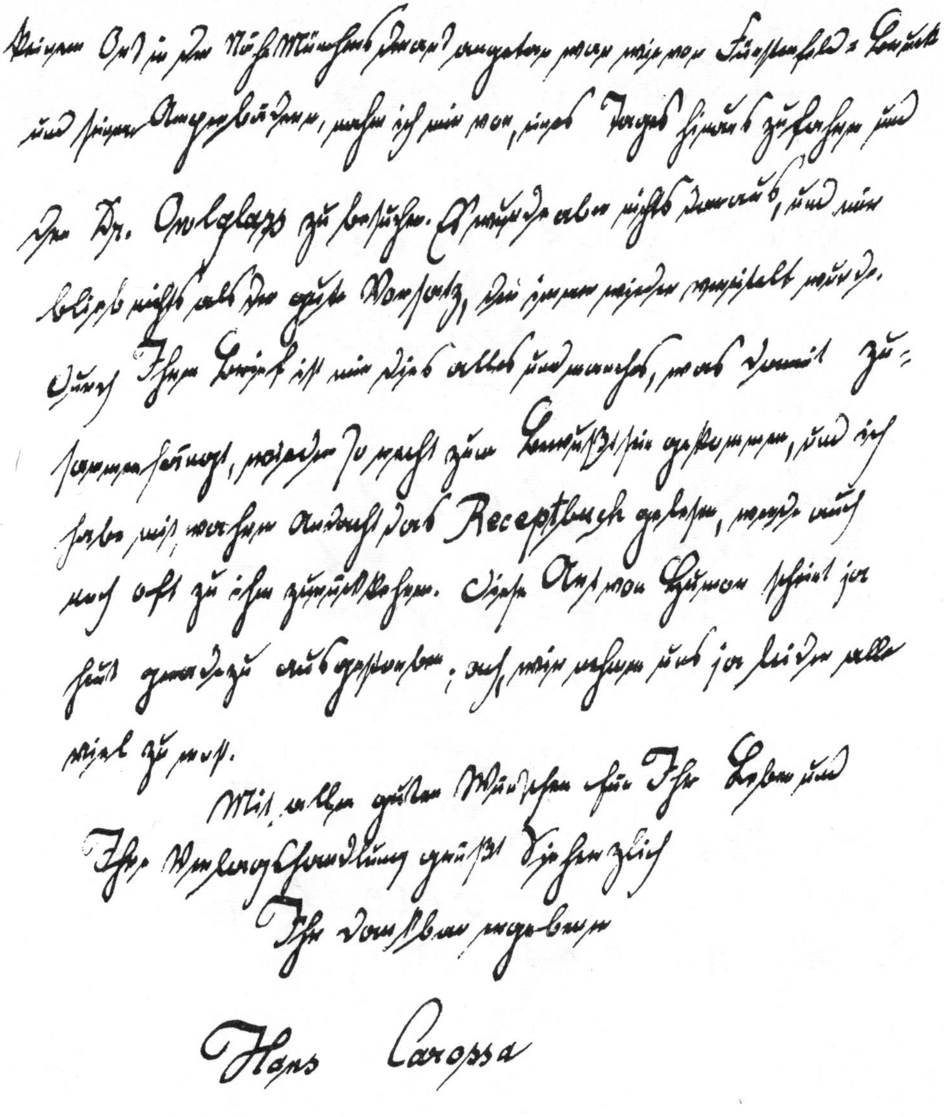

seinen Ort in der Nähe Münchens durch Angaben [illegible] wie von Fürstenfeld-Bruck
und seinen Angestellten, nahm ich mir vor, eines Tages hinaus zu fahren und
den Dr. Owlglass zu besuchen. Es wurde aber nichts daraus, und mir
blieb nichts als der gute Vorsatz, der immer wieder verschoben wurde.
Durch Ihren Brief ist mir dies alles und manches, was damit zu-
sammenhängt, wieder so recht zum Bewußtsein gekommen, und ich
habe mit wahrer Andacht das Receptbuch gelesen, werde auch
noch oft zu ihm zurückkehren. Diese Art von Humor scheint ja
heute geradezu ausgestorben; auch wir nehmen uns ja leider alle
viel zu ernst.
Mit allen guten Wünschen für Ihr Leben und
Ihre Verlagshandlung grüßt Sie herzlich
Ihr dankbar ergebener
Hans Carossa

Page of a letter written by Hans Carossa

Frage und Antwort

„ der die Welt erfuhr
faltig und ergraut,
Narb an Narbenspur
auf gefurchter Haut,

den die Not geletzt,
den der Dämon trieb —
sage, was zuletzt
dir verblieb."

„ Was aus Schmerzen kam,
war Vorübergang.
Und mein Ohr vernahm
nichts als Lobgesang."

Werner Bergengruen

appears in Carossa's works, in which he follows up the labyrinthine tracks of
life and suffering, as a symbol of the great unknown.

In this connection we must be content to mention only a selection of names.
Werner Bergengruen — like Baron Otto von Taube who has written delightful
stories and reminiscences of his youth — is a Baltic German who bears eloquent
witness in favour of a world which has disappeared since the first world war.
The natural obscurity of the human soul, which we tend either to drag out
into the light by force or else to plumb with the mind, is to him familiar ground.
He accepts it as an inevitable and inherent part of our being, neither violating
it nor unduly dramatizing it. In all his books, both those evincing a classical
clarity as well as those with romantic intricacies, the roles are fairly distributed
between the forces of light and the forces of darkness. This poised and tolerant
attitude is most uncharacteristic of our time. It may be that the very gifts
which Bergengruen possesses and reveals as a story-teller of charm and humour,
with a shrewdness which resolves the most intricate plot in the twinkling of
an eye and a wisdom content with its own knowledge of what is right — that
these gifts are so much coveted as an antidote that Bergengruen's popularity
is that of the writer who proclaims something which just at that moment no
one has been expecting to hear.

Werner Bergengruen, drawing by Gerda von Stengel

Post-war Literature

Literature in a divided country

There are certain rather special aspects which must be taken into account when studying the situation of German literature since the end of the last war. To begin with it should be remembered that the expression 'German literature' already began to acquire a slightly ambiguous meaning during the period of the Third Reich, since it was applied equally to writers within the national frontiers and those who wrote in exile or as emigrants in other parts of the world. After 1945, however, there came a definite split. Apart from Ricarda Huch, who died soon after the war, the venerable figure of Gerhart Hauptmann and Thomas Mann as a genuine intellectual authority, no German author has yet enjoyed full recognition in both the eastern and the western parts of the

The problem of Brecht

former Reich. The case of Bertolt Brecht is an exception because Germans in the west differentiate between the artistic value of his works and the dogma which they propound, while it is not absolutely certain whether unqualified appreciation of Brecht is even permissible in the eastern zone. An objective evaluation of Brecht's work as a whole is impossible at the moment because objectivity is in contradiction to the deeper intent of his works and because it would be equally wrong to let the discrepancy existing between his dogma and political practice speak either for him or against him. If we regard it as being in his favour, we inevitably make a Utopian of him. If we take it as a negative factor we brand him as a false prophet. Neither verdict is justified.

The ideological coercion exercised by authoritarian regimes makes it very difficult for outsiders to judge whether writers on the other side of the Iron Curtain remain at their posts in order to preserve what they can in the intellectual field, or whether they should be regarded as exponents of the regime.

Even if we felt certain of our conclusions in some cases, it might be very dangerous for those concerned to be praised by the wrong side. The mere fact that their works were looked upon with favourable interest on this side of the Iron Curtain would be sufficient to arouse suspicion of subversive intentions on the part of the writer. This is the situation which has to be faced. There can be no compromise between freedom and bondage. There is no clearer proof of this than the fact that a tyrannical regime will not even condone the expression of spontaneous approval; in fact, if a writer living within its dominion achieves genuine popularity at home, it immediately views his merits as suspect. Dictators have always distrusted public opinion.

We must therefore limit ourselves to a discussion of West German literature. We may just mention that Arnold Zweig, whose novel *Der Streit um den Sergeanten Grischa* was the most important of the war novels published in the nineteen-twenties, has settled in the eastern zone; that Leonhard Frank has again professed his faith in the socialist system in the other part of Germany, and the great narrative power of Anna Seghers is also appreciated in the West. Among the lyric poets, special mention should be made of Peter Huchel.

These are by no means all the problems to be faced, however. In normal circumstances a literary period sees the artistic production of the older generation achieve its climax, while the rising generation either carries on the tradition of its elders or attacks it. In times of crisis a radical break may occur between the generations, such as was the case in Germany after the first world war. The situation after the second world war is entirely different.

The postponed clash between the younger and older generations

The elder generation is split within itself. There is the literary production of the emigrants, of which only a small part is known and which has still not fully penetrated our minds, and there is the literary production of the writers who published books in Germany under the Third Reich, which by no means implies voluntary submission to the regime.

It is necessary to touch on this point because as a result of the split mentioned above the normal process of succeeding generations has suffered from a dual distortion. Every generation settles accounts with the preceding one and the point of departure in this case was total catastrophe. Hence it was natural that this should lead to an equally complete and drastic settlement of accounts. Meanwhile the literature which had been produced beyond the frontiers of the Third Reich and was only gradually becoming known had still to be considered. The

An impossible alliance

discussion of this literature was complicated by the fact that the younger generation at first tended to regard the authors who had openly declared their hostility to the regime and predicted its downfall as allies. It only gradually came to realize that these too belonged to another generation, that it was impossible to take up the threads which had been broken by the split in 1933, and that a genuine alliance with its predecessors was in the long run quite out of the question.

The appreciation of contemporary literature in other countries

The situation remained unclarified for a long time, while contacts were resumed with the foreign literature of Europe and America. It must be remembered that in many cases this was the first opportunity for German writers to become acquainted with literary phenomena such as Joyce and Proust, figures like Henry James or Virginia Woolf, or more recently Frank Kafka, Thomas Wolfe, Ernest Hemingway, John Steinbeck and William Faulkner, whose works were already the subject of critical discussion and appreciation in other countries. Thus the great post-war literary discussion was carried on over a very wide sector. Kafka, who had started to write before the first world war and whose works had been the subject of lively discussion in Arthur Kutscher's literature class in Munich in the nineteen-thirties — by a generation, of course, which was decimated in the war — suddenly became of such topical interest that the fact that this was a case of rejuvenation and revival of an author's literary production passed unnoticed. Robert Musil and the Swiss Robert Walser were still unknown to us at that time. Yet how important they are to the understanding of Kafka. Thomas Mann had announced his return with *Doktor Faustus*, Hermann Hesse with his late work *Das Glasperlenspiel*. Hermann Kasack, who had experienced the literary battles of the early 'twenties in Berlin at close quarters, published the novel *Die Stadt hinter dem Strom*, in which the past, in fact the whole of our civilization, was transposed into the realm of the shades. A native of Hamburg, Hans Erich Nossack, who lived in the same house as Kasack in Potsdam at the end of the war, wrote a dream-like, visionary tale entitled *Nekyia*, after the book of the Odyssey which describes the descent of Ulysses into Hades. Elisabeth Langgässer, whose last novel had been followed by years of silence, made her appearance again with the apocalyptic novel *Das Unauslöschliche Siegel*.

Great novels of the post-war period: Hermann Kasack, Elisabeth Langgässer

Apocalyptic authors

In spite of the differences in subjects, style and underlying attitude of these novels, as well as in the stage of maturity of their writers, they all revealed a common feature: the conviction that the visions and hopes which earlier generations had cherished of the future had proved illusory. The problem which had occupied Hermann Hesse during his whole life: how to achieve one's own consummation while simultaneously serving an association or community of like-minded fellows — which was the underlying theme of his story *Die Morgenland-fahrt* — was introduced again in *Das Glasperlenspiel* in a more urgent form, making the stern judgment on our time, technology and civilization appear convincing. Thomas Mann's answer to Nietzsche's conception of genius, in *Doktor Faustus*, which was inspired by a personal crisis only completely overcome later, in his speech on Schiller, could be taken as directed at the whole of German culture. Elisabeth Langgässer's procedure was still more revolutionary, bursting open the innerworldly structure of the novel and directly exposing reality to the powers of damnation and mercy, conceived in the most real sense. That Kasack's Hades was also the world of imagination into which modern writing plunges ever more deeply, and that similarly Hans Erich Nossack, in his *Interview mit dem Tode,* went out in pursuit of lost myth, tracking it down to depths where it became doubtful whether it would be possible — as Thomas Mann had wished — to humanize it, are considerations of only secondary importance by comparison with the first impression of a lost future.

Those who no longer see a promise in the future turn for compensation to the past. In this case, however, not the historical or chronological past which proceeds straight ahead from one period to the next, but the infinite form of the past which is made available to us in literature. When the writer discovers in literature the infinite dimension in which alone his creative activity can realize its own essential truth — the truth which relieves him of the obligation of being present or responsible as author — a new state of consciousness is born. This only apparently corresponds to the expressionist state of consciousness. For although the expressionist may have regarded subjective experience as merely an opportunity to cross over into the objective medium of the painting or the poem, the moment of passage from the subjective to the objective was unique and irreplaceable. In speaking of the expressionist drama we stated that the artist of that period believed he was living at the zenith of time, while never before had

Cover designed by Martin Kausche

The infinite dimension of literature

such authoritative value been attributed to the present. The visions which Hans Henny Jahnn, Georg Kaiser, Ernst Toller and the youthful Brecht adapted for the theatre, and the Utopian visions of Alfred Döblin and Robert Musil, all testify to their authors' belief that their own time would be the starting point of a great new era. The plays of the Swiss Friedrich Dürrenmatt, on the other hand, are dramatic commentaries on situations and conflicts the time and location of which remain undefined. Brecht's 'epic drama' requires the 'master' as didactic figure (as in Max Frisch's much discussed play *Andorra*). If an author does not wish to commit himself to an ideology he may replace the teacher by a kind of master of ceremonies.

Page of Georg Kaiser's manuscript: 'Die Bürger von Calais'

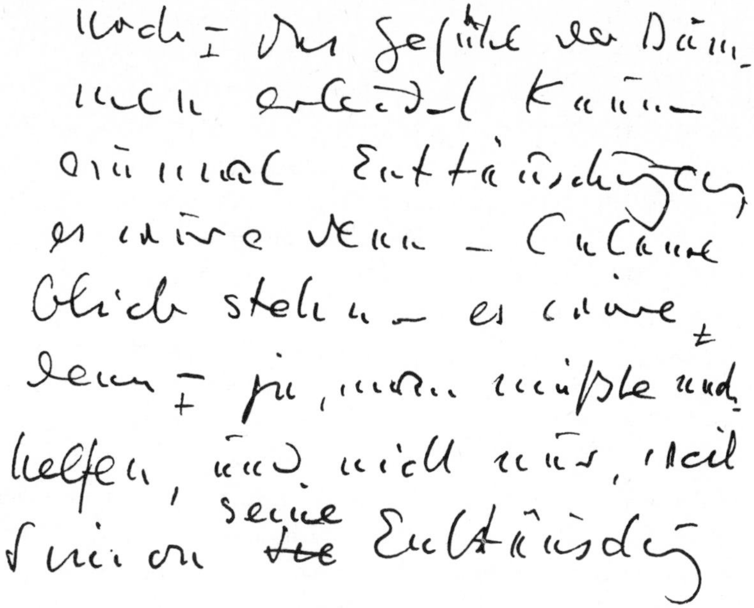

Stefan Andres' handwriting

Futuristic consciousness has disappeared in post-war literature. The play *Draussen vor der Tür* by Wolfgang Borchert, who died young, is typical of the disillusionment felt with regard to the promises of history. Wolfgang Hildesheimer shows dramatic intelligence. It may occasionally appear as if expressionistic tendencies had survived the catastrophe, particularly in the case of older writers such as Elisabeth Langgässer, Stefan Andres, Johannes Urzidil and others. However, in such cases the forward-looking tendencies of expressionism are weakening or being superseded by moralizing conclusions. This dilemma appears clearly in Klaus Mann's *Alexander* novel. Stefan Andres' *Utopia* is no more than a secret password used for mutual identification among a widely scattered group of like-minded authors. It no longer represents the vital resolution of a generation. The great novel *Die Sintflut* in which Andres gives a comprehensive picture of the cultural catastrophe, takes an esoteric turn in the last volume, *Der graue Regenbogen*. This was inevitable. We have seen how Hermann Broch realized the increasingly cryptographic nature of his novel *Der Tod des Vergil* and how

Stefan Andres

Hermann Hesse could only escape from the world of 'Kastalia' by making a determined leap for freedom.

In speaking of the infinite aspect of literature I do not mean its universality. Universality is always referred to a central point. The infinite quality remains intact as a cosmic whole even where the expressionist does not enter into the invisible realm with his work, but holds back in order not to endanger its inviolable order. In his *Glasperlenspiel* Hesse laid the greatest emphasis on the value of objectivity. What the game requires of its adepts is neither originality nor genius, but contemplation and self-forgetfulness. Its elements are to be found in all spheres of human activity, thought and creative work, regardless of their period or cultural context. Similarly, the action which temporarily links together these various elements is of immediate interest only in connection with the game and not historically speaking. We get the impression, however, that as Hesse himself continued to play his game of beads, reducing it to an ever purer form, he gradually began to tire of the game and its infinite character. In the end it seemed to him to conceal no more than the arrogance of idle knowledge, estrangement from reality and aversion to new contacts of a civilization grown old and wise but also infirm, barring the way to a successor.

The game of beads, which Hesse occasionaly associated with the dream of a *Mathesis univeralis,* is really playing with infinity. As soon as we submit the treasures of our intellectual culture indiscriminately to the ingenuity of talent, this culture takes on an infinite quality: it no longer has either beginning or end and enters the round of current, topical possibilities.

If we survey the literature of the post-war period as a whole we discover many signs which would seem to indicate that in it the infinite dimension of literature has been discovered, in the same sense as André Malraux has discovered the 'imaginary museum' of sculpture.

To summarize: The fact that future horizons are now barred has led to the conception of literature no longer as a space to be peopled with images of a future man, but rather as a domain of infinite extension in all directions. Not long after the war, Jean Gebser spoke of the 'aperspective view of the world', which had already superseded the perspective view of the world in the arts some time before. The question arises whether man's will to determine his place in the

Hesse as gardner
Caricature by H. U. Steger

future is also part of the perspective or whether it has been lost as the immediate locus of self-determination together with the perspective. We shall try to find the answer.

Since German literature tends, as we have repeatedly emphasized in this analysis, to attribute the greatest importance to the matter of education, or — more generally speaking — to the question of how far the individual can realize his own potentialities in the world, it it inevitable that in times of anarchy it must either prove that society and our environment are responsible for hampering our self-realization, or else prove that the individual is the product of his position and circumstances.

Both cases are preceded by an examination of conscience or, as the Austrian writer Herbert Eisenreich expresses it in the title of one of his short stories, the individual is invited to 'live more clearly'. In so far we are justified in saying that the writer is conscious of his time, that he has understood what the situation demands and interprets his mission with restraint in accordance with the fatality of a situation which imposes limitations on him at every turn. Thomas Mann predicted at the end of the war that we were about to embark on a moral era. If Ortega is right in his assertion that man feels compelled to do from a sense of duty that which he is no longer inspired to do by illusion and imagination, we should have an explanation for the extremely restricted world which we discover in post-war literature.

Lyric poetry

Moral and methodical restriction

What is to be understood by the restricted world and restricted action of the poet is best illustrated by considering lyric poetry. The restriction has a dual cause. First, the poet avoids everything that might place him in the debt of reality; this is the moral aspect. Secondly, he takes care that his poetic diction shall come up to the standard he has set himself; this is the methodical aspect.

In Germany, people generally do not understand if someone talks about 'method' in connection with poetry. There is a deep-rooted belief that the words and songs of a poet flow spontaneously from the depths of his heart. Method is appropriate to science, we are told. Science aims at securing rational results, and to achieve this end it uses methodical procedures, the different stages of which can be generally followed and imitated. The foundations of poetry, on the other hand, are personal experience and intuition, so that it is quite superfluous to seek a method.

Poetic method

The objection is justified up to a certain point. However, everyone is bound to admit that the experience or intuition, or whatever else we consider to be the 'essence' of the poem, is at first not present in verbal form, and that in order to put it into words the poet has to make a certain effort. This effort by which he captures and clothes his original, subjective inspiration for a poem in an objective structure of words is what we refer to as the poet's method.

Naturally, this method must not be conceived as based on fixed notions or as merely joining up two points by a straight line. On the contrary, it allows the inspiration full scope as the image or experience is transposed into the medium of language. The term 'method' is only inappropriate if we take it to mean something clearly defined and binding. In our time, however, even physicists no longer give the term such a strictly defined meaning; they speak of analogy and symbols in connection with method and their interpretation allows a certain scope to the phenomena concerned.

Wilhelm Lehmann, whose poetic intuition places him closest to Oskar Loerke, has spoken of the 'flexible order' of life and poetry in contrast to the rigid order of a system. The 'flexible order' is not final and does not determine the phenomenon. It indicates the natural law which governs it, which is not isolated or defined in any substantial form, but which manifests itself in mutual relationship with other phenomena. The V formation of wild geese in flight is not an abstract sign, identical only with itself, but is determined by the air-resistance, by the beating of the birds' wings, by economy of motive power within the group, etc. If we consider the V formation as component element of a flexible order, we involuntarily think of analogies ranging from the keel of a ship to the battle order of an army in the field. That is to say: we realize that the 'flexible order' of language and mental imagery is analogous to the flexible order which embraces all natural phenomena. Hence the poet should endeavour to imitate this flexible relationship of natural phenomena metaphorically as closely as possible.

Wilhelm Lehmann and the 'flexible order'

A perfectly harmonious relationship between the mobility of natural phenomena and the zone of resonance of language is found in the myth. The myth and the folk-tale do not represent a definite or fixed order but one which is constantly evolving and fulfilling itself. According to Lehmann's conception, the poem reflects the myth once more as in a drop of water. It not only reflects, however, but also absorbs as tendency a movement which is unceasingly striving towards completion. Since this movement takes place in language, however, relationships become ever more subtle, associations more elusive and points of contact rarer.

Folk-tale and myth

The preceding observations are applicable to Lehmann's poetry in which — by contrast to that of Loerke — the optical element rather than the acoustical is dominant. Comparing this poetry with that of Hermann Hesse we notice how much more restrained it is in subjective content. Hesse enters into his subject phenomena as poet and then withdraws from them again. He celebrates the great moment of unity, only to be found again at the end standing in the shadows, excluded, solitary and yearning. This alternating rhythm of amalgamation and exclusion, fulfilment and unsatisfied longing is particularly noticeable running

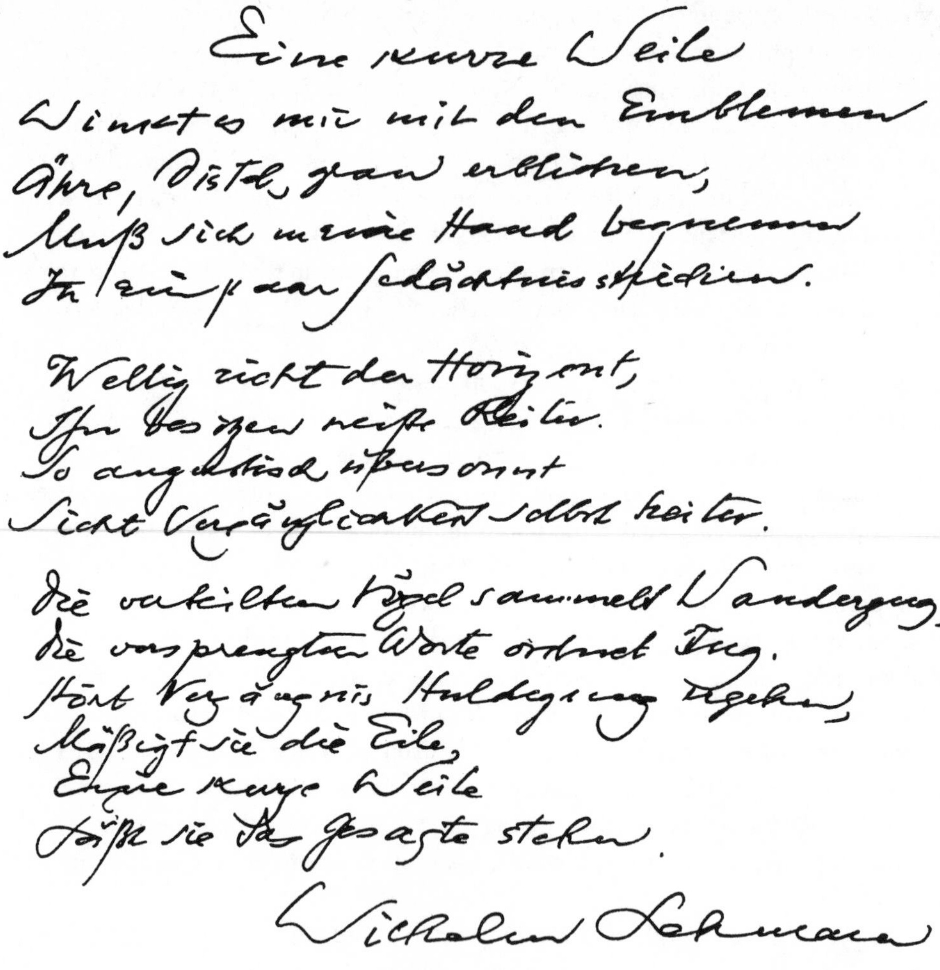

Eine kurze Weile
Winkt es mir mit den Emblemen
Ähre, Distel, grau erblichen;
Muß sich in meine Hand begrenzen
In ein paar Gedächtnisstücken.

Wellig zieht der Horizont,
Ihn bestreut reiße Reiter.
So angstlos überkommt
Sicht Vergänglichkeit selbst heiter.

Die verkühlten Vögel sammelt Wanderung,
Die versprengten Worte ordnet Tag.
Hört Verzögnis Huldigung begehen,
Mäßigt sie die Eile,
Eine kurze Weile
Läßt sie das Gesagte stehen.

Wilhelm Lehmann

Hesse's lyric works through the cycle of poems which are the lyrical interpretation of the *Glasperlenspiel.*

We have spoken of a 'restricted world' This could mean that the reality of the world to-day so gravely clips the wing of Lehmann's 'flexible order' that the poet fears to allow himself a luxury at the expense of reality. It could also mean, however, that the poet has come to realize that language, inasmuch as it is poetic language, is irreconcilable with reality in any form, and therefore limits himself to the restricted scope of the poetic. Both tendencies are evident in the poetry of the post-war period.

Handwriting of Georg von der Vring

When poetic inspiration comes into collision with discordant aspects of reality, the hymnic note gives way to one of lament. The song of praise alternates with the elegy in Rilke's *Duineser Elegien.* The underlying note of Marie Luise Kaschnitz's poetry is one of lamentation. Werner Bergengruen celebrates in an ode the beauty of the universe at the moment of its decline. Elisabeth Langgässer preserves her visions in the mystic crystal of form. Georg von der Vring seeks the enduring in song, as it shines forth untarnished in Shakespeare's tragedies. Rudolf Hagelstange's yearning for a beauty worthy of mankind is clothed in the spirit of form.

The poem here reveals a different kind of unity in each case, but unity and a form complete in itself is still intended. Another class of poems exists, however, the common feature of which is the absence of a definite form.

Critical poetry   In an essay *Kommentare zu Gedichten von Brecht,* Walter Benjamin illustrated the nature of critical poetry by an example. The city-dweller who only sees trees growing occasionally, in back courtyards, regards them as purely formal representatives of an order from which he, as lodger or tenant of a flat, is excluded. The poet addresses the tree, thinking of its predecessors which still grew and flourished in close contact with nature. He does not address it in a tone of intimacy, however, but in a more distant, formal manner which expresses the fact that there are things happening in the world at present that are of greater importance to the poet than all poetic conventions. For instance, the fact that the house-owner asserts an unconditional claim to the tree, thus reducing it simply to a material possession, may constitute a state of affairs which it is the poet's duty to criticise rather than to avoid by closing his eyes to the false, existing order and escaping back to an order which no longer exists. The urge to determine the real facts of a case manifests itself particularly when a period of exaggerated or over-effusive expressions of sentiment is succeeded by one of more balanced and sober taste. As Hermann Broch convincingly explained, hypertrophy is bound to occur eventually in any circumscribed order. The day comes when it is forcibly broken asunder and the perceptive faculty once more takes its bearings directly from reality. The feeling for the whole is lost, but life gains a new horizon.

Our astonishment at the fact that, in spite of everything, poetry is still written, is perhaps the most convincing proof of the vitality of certain poems which have been published since the war. What is meant by 'in spite of everything' need hardly be explained. The substance of poetry has been corroded by the fact that the word *Buchenwald* no longer means simply a beech-forest, as it did, but conjures up the image of a concentration camp. The forest is robbed of its innocence. It is remarkable that poems are possible all the same, that is to say honest poems, facing up to the reality unmasked and standing the test of this confrontation. To attempt a classification of post-war poetry at the present time would be premature. We must simply consider the poems in the order in which they came to our notice. In 1948 Günter Eich published a volume of poems entitled *Abgelegene Gehöfte*, in which certain features of the new poetry were clearly evident: images not introduced by consecutive thought but fixed by word-combinations; the sceptical reflection of former moods in face of a reality no longer susceptible of moods; restriction to the here and now; toning down of the language to a level at which it again becomes receptive for reality. In spite of being purged of so many traditional attributes, Eich's poetry retained its vital force. Indeed, captivity, hunger, the complete uncertainty as to whence and whither made of it a necessity as essential as bread and water.

Poetic production continues in spite of what has happened

Günter Eich

Eich's second volume of poems is called *Botschaften des Regens*. Here the horizon is widened, though still dark. 'Messages' are only received in the sphere of poetic self-interrogation.

Critical discussion with predecessors and the development of individual tendencies only appear at a second stage. Both phases are recognizable in the poems of Karl Krolow. To begin with, the poem, regaining its casual aspect, is a commodity: knife or tin-opener. It serves a purpose, without the poet's having to worry about whether what he produces has any value or is of use to others. The man in a prisoner's camp who finds a bit of wood and starts carving designs on it does not worry either whether there is any real value in what he is doing. This is what I mean by 'restriction'. In all probability, poetry is thus restricted to the function which it had in primaeval times, when it was still an intimate component of everyday life. In a note on his *Lyrikbuch der Jahrhundertmitte* Walter Höllerer states that the modern folk-tale is familiar with imminent danger. 'Folk-tale' seems to me already too pretentious a name for that which Höllerer

Cover for Günter Eich's 'Abgelegene Gehöfte' Woodcut by Karl Rössing

has in mind. Charms and incantations murmured to oneself in the hope of averting impending peril cannot be regarded as tales to be told to others. It is true that the symbolists — and before them Poe — like George and Schröder in Germany, also played with the musical sound of vowels; but the tone they produced was of exquisite quality. As far as I know, no one has yet drawn attention to the fact that the lines which children recite or sing while playing their round games are often quoted in narrative fiction to emphasize the aspect of emptiness and infinity underlying the action. This is the case in Gerd Gaiser's first novel *Eine Stimme hebt an*, in *Tauben im Gras* by Wolfgang Koeppen, in

Freies Geleit

> Mit schlaftrunkenen Vögeln
> und winddurchschossenen Bäumen
> steht der Tag auf, und das Meer
> leert einen schäumenden Becher auf ihn.
>
> Die Flüsse wallen ans große Wasser,
> und das Land legt Liebesversprechen
> der reinen Luft in den Mund
> mit frischen Blumen.
>
> Die Erde will keinen Rauchpilz tragen,
> kein Geschöpf ausspeien vorm Himmel,
> mit Regen und Zornesblitzen abschaffen
> die unerhörten Stimmen des Verderbens.

Ingeborg Bachmann's handwriting

antwort des fabelwesens

Der Drache hat sich mit der Nelke vermählt
um dich zu erzeugen
irgends lebst du, das ist
wo die Kralle ausschlägt im März
um zu blühen
wo der oktoberne Donner zart
und zu Duft wird. ruf!
ich will zu dir kommen,
sag mir wohin,
damit wir einander befragen
und lieben können,
furchtlose Freude,
und gut sein? –

Handwriting of H. M. Enzensberger

– gut sein ist nirgends'

the plays of Max Frisch and in O. F. Walter's *Herr Tourel*. Hans Magnus Enzensberger has published a collection of children's verse.

It would be a great mistake to label these phenomena as belonging to the magic arts; such exalted and far-fetched terms are not appropriate to the restricted world of the modern poem. But play is still allowed in that world. Christian Morgenstern, who took Nietzsche's reproach about 'deadly earnest' to heart and produced delightful and profound nonsense in his *Galgenlieder*, and Joachim Ringelnatz, who never ran after ideas but let the ideas lead him by the hand, have their successors in Günter Grass, Hans Magnus Enzensberger (who gives a polemical point to the idea), Walter Höllerer in *Zerstreuung eines Fischs*, and others. The free zone of adventure lying between the realm of symbols and the workshops of the technical world allows the use of former allegorical images and the conversion of technical processes into a playful element. Here we may mention the poems of Karl Krolow. Weakening of the poetic impulse inevitably results in the intensification of the artistic side. Heinz Piontek's poetry retains an epic rhythm and does not lose sight of the limiting boundaries.

The topsy-turvy world

The zone of adventure is, however, also poetry's point of departure for its journey into the realm of imagination. Reading Ingeborg Bachmann's radio play *Der gute Gott von Manhattan*, we find, on closer examination, that her poetry

Journey into imaginary regions

INGEBORG
BACHMANN
ANRUFUNG
DES
GROSSEN
BÄREN

GEDICHTE

PIPER

Cover designed by Gerhard M. Hotop

is tuned not to the possible but to the impossible. It would be hardly admissible, however, to draw a sharp distinction between the impossibility of living and the impossibility of writing poetry. This distinction was very marked in Gottfried Benn because he had experienced the departure of the natural sciences into the realm of the imaginary and always remained conscious of the empirical coast which had offered him a firm footing as a doctor and scientist, in short as empiricist. The Italian poet Corrado Alvaro wrote in his diary that the erotic acquires an almost exclusive value to the same degree as social ties decay. In Robert Musil's novel, the second part — which tells the story of a love which is exclusive and absolute — fulfils this compensating role in relation to the first part, the story of the 'parallel plot' which gives Ulrich the opportunity of displaying a whole series of distinctive qualities without committing himself. The erotic — or let us say love — is the last of all human aspirations which still maintains its claim to be absolute. And in so doing it proves its own impossibility. The very heights to which it soars show how great will be its fall. Or else its descent into hell shows us that the only counterpart of the absolute which we still possess is to be seen in eternal damnation. But this situation applies equally to language, if it aspires to absolute poetic purity. By renouncing every possibility it may succeed in expressing the emptiness of its impossibility in a framework of words. Or on the other hand it may plunge into the abyss and find in vanity, separation, utter destitution and recurring torment the ciphers of that impotent infinity to which not even words can cling for ever.

In the poetry of Paul Celan we are dragged down into this chasm. There is always a dual object: the dissolution of reality and the dissolution of language, the anonymity of which is exposed at ever deeper levels. In the poem *Todesfuge* we find eddying splinters of verse which are no man's speech but only the recurring announcement of a message, signposts in the continuously narrowing funnel of fate.

Nelly Sachs   We cannot close this chapter without mentioning Nelly Sachs, who suffered the fate of the Jewish people and found refuge in Sweden. Her poems *Flucht und Verwandlung* appeared in Germany in 1959. We spoke of the restricted world and restricted action which are to be regarded in poetry as proof of its sincerity and straightforward tendency. This also implies being accessible to death and exposing language to non-existence. Yet the poems of Nelly Sachs differ in one essential point from most other modern poems. Although they hurry past, homeless and flying from horrors, the wide range which they encompass becomes apparent once more just as they disappear from sight. Ingeborg Bachmann also sometimes succeeds in imparting this feeling, but with her the heralding voice has a touch of the prophetic. She transposes the world to a new beginning, after its constellations have set and its fruits decayed. But the ending and rebirth of a world are only an instant beside the eternal voice which is heard from beyond the horizon of time and resounds in the poetry of declining ages.

Narrative fiction

The comprehensive term 'narrative fiction' already implies a concession. Formerly a sharp distinction was made between different categories, such as the novel and the short story or prose fiction and poetry. To-day only writers who have retained the fine sense of a former age and hierarchical order for what is proper pay any attention to the characteristic features expected of a certain species. Thomas Mann used to speak of what was 'proper'. Werner Bergengruen refers to this innate sense of decorum as "the knowledge of what is fitting", in recollection of a line from Goethe's *Westöstlicher Divan*. His latest book, *Der dritte Kranz*, is a classic example of highly developed narrative art. The style, however, betrays that the differentiation involved in such development goes hand in hand with a certain old-fashioned trait, and the writer then observes his own diction with irony. A masterful illustration of this principle was given by Thomas Mann in his novel *Der Erwählte*.

The ironic accent is seldom heard in post-war literature. Wolf von Niebelschütz in his novel *Der blaue Kammerherr*, Kurt Kusenberg in his short stories and Klaus Nonnemann in his collection of narratives *Vertraulicher Geschäftsbericht* provide examples of it. Humour is more frequent, as witness Arno Schmidt, Wolfdietrich Schnurre, Martin Walser, Günter Grass. The ironical style is a romantic category and is nearly always found in conjunction with romantic echoes. Thomas Mann paid homage to it if only through his admiration for Nietzsche and Richard Wagner. Hermann Hesse cannot be imagined without his romantic predecessors. Musil's irony is reminiscent of the serene, crushing irony of Friedrich Schlegel. Bergengruen loves the flourishes and fantasy of E. T. A. Hoffmann.

There is something theatrical about irony, an aspect which was dealt with by Kierkegaard and did not fail to attract Nietzsche's malicious comments. Making

Cover designed by Imre Reiner

use of different artistic forms, alternating between various styles, the game of hide-and-seek in which, in order not be caught, the writer conceals himself behind a dummy author, are all ironical devices. They are to be found in the literature of other countries too, in the works of André Gide, Unamuno and Gómez de la Serna, Aldous Huxley and Evelyn Waugh. The humorist, on the other hand, leaves no doubt from the beginning that the double of the 'I', who appears *in corpore,* is a caricature.

Ironic artifice is as seldom found in post-war literature as is psychological finesse. The basic form, which remains evident even when the plot combines several structural elements, is the story. This means 'story' as opposed to 'narrative' which implies the person of the narrator as well as a circle of listeners with whom contact is established through the expressive medium of style. The story tells itself, which does not mean, however, that it may not be told in the first person or in the form of a mental monologue, or that the plot may not be divided into components which can be viewed in perspective. For this, in fact, merely confirms the independence of the story from the person of the narrator or listener, and the fact that its only valid motive is that it takes place within language. The 'I' which speaks to itself in the monologue is no more the 'I' of the narrator than the artificial interconnection of the parts is intrigue in the traditional sense of the word.

The 'story' or plot

In his *Vorschule der Ästhetik* Jean Paul recommended the novelist to lay his mines at the beginning of his work, ready for explosion at the end. This cunning practice of mine-laying with a view to the brilliant display of fireworks in the last chapter, which the reader anticipates with interest, is only very rarely to be found in the post-war novel. One who still knows the trick of it is Heimito von Doderer, who in his novel *Die Strudlhofstiege* ingeniously exploits the confusion of identity resulting from the mutual resemblance of a pair of twin sisters. Even here, however, the intrigue is not really introduced for the benefit of the reader. The case of mistaken identity is intended rather to suggest that society having lost all sense of order has also lost the faculty of distinguishing between the true and the false; thus, for instance, it no longer sees the difference between a film-star and a reigning queen. This phenomenon also provided Hermann Kasack with the subject of his novel *Fälschungen.* The mistaken identity

The novelist and his 'fireworks'

Heimito von Doderer

Frauen halten den Mann, der sie geheiratet hat, für mindestens incompetent, wenn nicht für schlimmeres. Das wird seine Gründe haben. Jedenfalls steht fest, dass Zihal ihr nichts sagte und auch von ihr nicht gefragt wurde. Beleg: sein 1927 getaner und ~~Jung Dr. Döllinger~~ diesfalls compotenter Bericht an Kajetan ~~durch Schno~~ über war er überhaupt sehr offenherzig und garnicht chinesisch.

Nun aber, Paula war inzwischen auch bei ihrem einstmaligen Chef in der Marc Aurel-Straße gewesen (wie sehen sie ja überhaupt tätig!). Aber mit einem noch geringeren Ergebnis als bei Zihal, eigentlich also mit garkeinem. Der Doctor Adler — man erinnert sich seiner vielleicht flüchtig aus dem Tennisclub Augarten — hatte eine so große Freude, als er Paula wiedersah, dass er ~~in seiner Kanzlei~~ (in seinem Arbeitszimmer) nur so um sie herumhüpfte und ehrlich glücklich war zu hören, sie habe einen lieben Mann und ein herziges Mäderl. Er wollte Bilder sehen und Paula war so klug gewesen, welche mitzubringen. Adler betrachtete die Photographien mit Entzücken, lief dazwischen hinaus, wo seine Klienten schon warteten, jedoch grüßend an diesen vorbei und in ~~das Zimmer~~ die Kanzlei wo seine Fräuleins saßen, deren eines er unter Vorstellungen der Dringlichkeit zum Blumenhändler und zum Conditor sprengte, von wo sie bald mit einem riesigen Strauss roter Rosen und einer Bonbonniere für eine kleine Fürstin zurück kam. Draußen wähnten die Fräuleins den Doctor acht verliebt, aber das war er garnicht, höchstens zeitweis (noch immer ~~in~~ in seine Frau.

Über die gegenständlichen Fragen Paula's ~~fuhr~~ (rüttelte) Adler rasch hinweg, ja erst hörte er ihr kaum zu, und ihre Fragen gingen in seinen viel zahlreicheren unter. Dazu muss man nun freilich halten, dass die

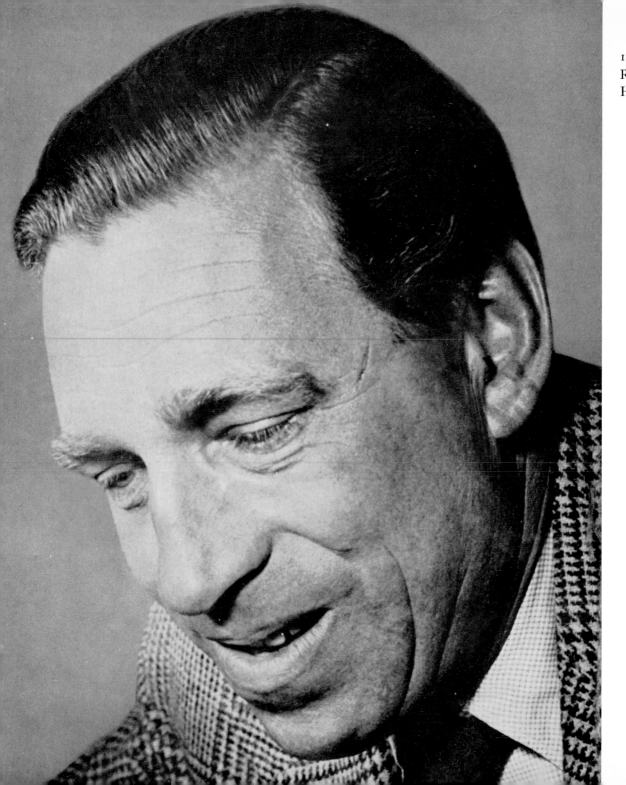

138
Heinrich
Böll

139
Hans Erich
Nossack

Arno Schmidt

Wolfdietrich Schnurre

Martin Walser

Kurt Kusenberg

142
Ingeborg
Bachmann

143
Marie Luise
Kaschnitz

Felix Hartlaub

Gerd Gaiser

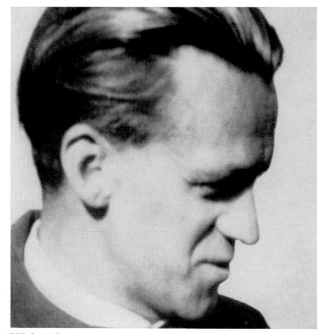

Walter Jens

Alfred Andersch

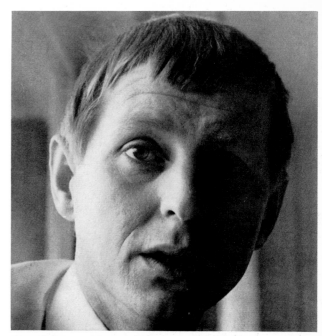

Hans Magnus Enzensberger

of the twin sisters is thus not so much intended to mislead the reader until the final denouement occurs as to indicate a shifting of values within society.

Of the writers living to-day, so far as I can see, Doderer is the only one who still understands how to deal with the structure, distribution of components and parallel execution of a polyphonic plot. His most important work up to the present, *Die Dämonen*—which is, however, quite equalled by his strictly composed prose pieces entitled *Divertimenti*—represents the novel in 'total' form. In *Die Strudlhofstiege* the plot still proceeds by stages, the characters make their entry, form groups, change places, complications occur. We have to imagine a stage-manager who arranges the groups, gives the cues and supervises the movements. In *Die Dämonen* the stage-manager has disappeared. The central focus of the plot is a public event, the announcement of which produces the most subtle changes in all strata of society and even in the atmosphere and appearance of the town. The writing of the work rises out of nothingness and having described a circle returns again to the void of the start.

The sweep of the circle depends on inventive energy or intensity, but also on the extent to which reality is still felt to be susceptible of assimilation. *Die Dämonen* could not have been written if Doderer had not seen, above all, Vienna and Viennese society spread out before his mind's eye like a living tissue of innumerable interwoven threads. The desire to organize a tangled complex into an orderly whole can only be inspired by the anticipation of that whole.

The novel is reduced to a mere story if the individual's view of life remains detached from all other views of life.

Occasionally we find separate stories combined in an aperspective relationship in post-war novels. Bruno E. Werner's novel *Die Galeere* and Hans Werner Richter's *Sie fielen aus Gottes Hand* may be mentioned in this connection. Wolfgang Koeppen, whose first novel *Eine unglückliche Liebe* appeared at the beginning of the 'thirties, has given us the oppressive picture of a German town just after the war in *Tauben im Gras*. The principle of demonstrating a state of chaos through disintegrated elements was suggested to him precisely by the lack of all connection and complete mutual isolation of the figures involved in his plot — the negro soldier belonging to the occupying forces, the impoverished girl of good family, the embittered widow of a Civil Servant, the intellectual, and the

Cover designed by Werner Rebhuhn

Aperspective novels

Wolfgang Koeppen

great poet from another country. The best novels of Luise Rinser *(Mitte des Lebens* and *Abenteuer der Tugend)* are dissociated biographical accounts.

Alfred Andersch

Alfred Andersch used a similar technique in *Sansibar oder der letzte Grund* in order to give a transcendency to the isolated element and transpose the action into the future dimension. It will be objected that this is futurism, but this does not altogether apply. Andersch's futurism is the result of separate perspectives which are mutually so exclusive that the point of coincidence towards which they tend appears as hypothetical as the intersection of two parallel lines at infinity. The vision was the futuristic form of expression in the nineteen-twenties; to-day, at best, it takes the form of experimental calculation. This observation also applies to the novels of Uwe Johnson, who has great linguistic talent: *Mutmassungen über Jakob* and *Das dritte Buch über Achim.*

Heinrich Böll

Heinrich Böll's novels are also based on the story. The fact that post-war authors — like the Italian neo-realists — have found inspiration in the American short story is interesting from the point of view of literary history but only of secondary importance as regards the fundamental standpoint. The French 'récit' has been a further source of inspiration. The transition from the self-contained story to the novel raises a number of technical problems. Since none of the actors appearing communicates with any of the others, as each one is enclosed in his own perspective, there are only two possibilities: either the story must be converted into structural material or it must be raised to a symbolic level. Just as the figure of the reading schoolboy in Andersch's novel has a symbolic function, the symbol being also, however, calculated and structurally designed as unifying point, Böll, in *Billard um halbzehn*, also combines the structural and the symbolizing processes. Rolf Schroers' novel *In fremder Sache* is related in structure.

There is naturally a whole complex of questions which arise in connection with this principle and which are not only topical in Germany but are a central theme of literary discussion in France, Italy, England, and in both the northern and southern states of America. These questions centre round the consideration that the writer, in endeavouring to remain loyal to his personal truth, may trespass against reality. In other words: in restricting the scope of his art, does he not also inadmissibly restrict reality? Walter Jens has brought out this point

Böll

Ansichten
eines Clowns

Roman
Kiepenheuer
& Witsch

most clearly as critic, although in his novels he rather tends to join the abstainers. In his novel *Stiller* Max Frisch dealt in a fascinating manner with the problem of the 'nobody'. We may put the concrete question: where is man at his work to be found in modern literature? It would seem as if the author now purposely sends his characters into retirement in order to be able to do what he wishes with them in accordance with his own idea of truth. Whether he locks them up in prison, turns them adrift on the ocean in a rubber dinghy or maroons them on an island, the reader always suspects that these precautions are taken in order to exclude any interference from direct reality. Innumerable examples could be quoted, but I shall only mention here those that have genuine artistic value: *Nichts in Sicht* by Jens Rehn, the stories *Templones Ende* by Martin Walser and *Sieg über die Dämmerung* by Gabriele Wohmann.

It is, however, important here to determine in each case whether the writer has succeeded by means of a bold stroke in introducing reality into his story, or whether he has merely made use of it to embellish an abstract plot. The stories *Geister und Leute* by Alfred Andersch are most ingenious strokes of reality. Herbert Eisenreich's stories *Böse schöne Welt* contain rich plunder from raids on a reality which has become exotic. Wolfdietrich Schnurre, Paul Schallück, Hans Scholz and Siegfried Lenz all capture reality, each with his own special snare. (The novels *Am grünen Strand der Spree* by Hans Scholz and *Ankunft Null Uhr Zwölf* by Paul Schallück are also virtually based on the story.)

The story is closer to the objective report than is the novel. The report, or account, is characterized by knowledge of the subject, reliable dating of facts, and concise diction. The diary, which is written with the intention of giving a quasi-photographic portrayal of the course of events, without any personal intervention by the writer, is an account which acquires a literary physiognomy only by virtue of its style. Felix Hartlaub's *Tagebuch aus dem Kriege*, written in Hitler's headquarters, is an account of this type, the style of which strikes a note between the matter-of-fact and the negligent. The diaries of Max Frisch should also be mentioned in this connection. A device used with particular mastery by Hans Erich Nossack is that of writing in the style of a report on a domain of which nothing is known to report. This principle is illustrated by the title under which he published a series of short stories: *Interview mit dem Tode*. The purpose

max Frisch

Stiller

Roman

Suhrkamp

Cover designed by Gunter Böhmer

The diary

The imaginary goal

Pen and ink drawing by Felix Hartlaub,
illustrating
'Geschichte vom Jungen' (1926)

of an interview is to gather facts. But we can gather no facts from death; we can only suffer it, and that strictly alone. However, as we indicated before, death is a cipher of the imaginary. The death of poor Milly in Henry James' novel allows James, who makes her die, to transfer the events which he describes ever further into the imaginary. In Nossack's case also the zone of the imaginary is extended by the movement of the plot towards death, the underworld and the virginity of Persephone. His tales are 'meetings in the antichamber', that is to say on the borders of the domain in which the venturing step becomes lost in the trackless region of the imaginary. His story *Unmögliche Beweisaufnahme* is in my opinion the best piece of narrative prose that has been published since the end of the war.

In Marie Luise Kaschnitz's stories too *(Lange Schatten)* the plot tends towards a pole which lies beyond the world of experience. The classical narrative form which normally stands out in relief, acquires, so to speak, a concave aspect which deflects the characters into the imaginary.

Another inhabitant of this border zone is Gerd Gaiser, a native of Swabia. In his case the imaginary zone is filled with memories which, withdrawn from reality, tend towards the nature of the primary image *(Das Schiff im Berg, Am Pass Nascondo)*. In his novel *Schlussball*, with great sensitivity and subtle modulations of style, he has woven stories together to form a plot of concentric structure.

We still have to take one more step and cross the border into the realm of pure imagination. This is sparsely populated. The leading figure is Arno Schmidt who has an impressive fund of ideas and vocabulary and is admirable in his invention of detail, though his plots are generally a little too rough-hewn. Among present-day writers he is the only one who has at his command the teeming vocabulary of the expressionists and boldly digs up vivid terms from remote strata of the language. Recently Günter Grass has attracted attention by two works which fall into the same category, a novel *Die Blechtrommel* and the story *Katz und Maus*. He also is being measured by a critical yardstick which is too short, if it does not reach back further than the 'twenties. The humorist generally looks back on a widely echelonned row of ancestors. It is no mere coincidence that Oskar, the drummer, who stopped growing when he was three, meets the

Cover designed by Gerhard M. Hotop

Men in the moon

Cover designed by Günter Grass

dwarf Narses who lived at the court of the emperor Justinian. The humorist loves the archaic because it confirms his prejudice against the material world. It gives no support to the illusion that material things can ever be anything other than what they are by nature. The rock is a fragment and the mantle of clouds under which we creep is our grandmother's skirts.

The critic must be content to trace certain lines; these may be effaced again once they have served their purpose of orientation. Many questions remain open. It is regrettable that these are not more discussed, and also by people not directly connected with the literary world like authors and intellectuals. Yet we have some distinguished critics, such as Friedrich Sieburg, Hans Egon Holthusen, Walter Jens, Curt Hohoff and Günter Blöcker, to mention but a few. One of these questions, which I wish to mention in conclusion, is the following: If the writer adheres strictly to the truth which he can answer for in the face of language — that is to say of his, the author's language, will he not inevitably risk the reproach that he is disregarding or even violating interests which many a reader expects him as a writer to defend? This is a genuine problem. One cannot simply tell the writer that he should look after the interests of his fellow-men and adapt his works accordingly, for this would mean depriving him of that truth which is only of value to us if he has found it by his own efforts and in his own language. On the other hand it would be just as wrong for the writer to refuse flatly to have due regard for the interests of his readers. Respect for the truth in art is the Alpha and Omega of any cultural policy. Respect for man — as he was, as he is or as he will be — helps the artist to overcome his isolation.

Appendix

Note

A study such as the present work must necessarily be selective. The names of many other authors of merit have had to be omitted. Readers desiring further information are referred to the following works:

Günter Blöcker	Die neuen Wirklichkeiten. Linien und Profile der modernen Literatur. Argon Verlag Berlin 1961
Hermann Friedmann/ Otto Mann	Deutsche Literatur im XX. Jahrhundert. Strukturen und Gestalten. Zwanzig Darstellungen. Rothe Verlag Hamburg 1959
Karl August Horst	Kritischer Führer durch die deutsche Literatur der Gegenwart. Nymphenburger Verlagshandlung München 1962
Walter Jens	Deutsche Literatur der Gegenwart. R. Piper & Co. Verlag München 1961
Albert Soergel/ Curt Hohoff	Dichtung und Dichter der Zeit. 2 Vols. August Bagel Verlag Düsseldorf 1961/63

Photographs: 17 *Thomas Mann*, Foto Thea Goldmann, Zürich. 18 *Nobel Prize for Thomas Mann*, Thomas Mann-Archiv, Zürich. 19 *Hermann Hesse*, Pressestelle des Börsenvereins Deutscher Verleger- und Buchhändler-Verbände e. V., Frankfurt/Main (Foto M. Hesse, Bern). 20 *Robert Musil*, Rowohlt Verlag, Reinbek. 21 *Alfred Döblin*, S. Fischer Verlag, Frankfurt/Main. 22 *Walter Hasenclever*, Schiller-Nationalmuseum, Marbach (Foto Riess, Berlin). 23 *Bertolt Brecht*, death-mask, Suhrkamp Verlag, Frankfurt/Main. 24 *Ferdinand Bruckner*, scene from "Die Verbrecher" (Foto Ilse Buhs, Berlin). 37 *Stefan George*, Süddeutscher Verlag, München, Bild-Archiv. 38 *Rainer Maria Rilke*, Insel-Verlag, Frankfurt/Main, published by permission of the Historisches Bild-Archiv Handke-Bernek. 39 *Franz Kafka*, S. Fischer Verlag, Frankfurt/Main. 40 *Rudolf Alexander Schröder*, Süddeutscher Verlag, München, Bild-Archiv. 41 *Ernst Jünger*, Ernst Klett Verlag, Stuttgart. 42 *Gerhart Hauptmann*, Schiller-Nationalmuseum, Marbach. 43 *Hugo von Hofmannsthal*, S. Fischer Verlag, Frankfurt/Main (Foto Ellinger, Salzburg). 44 *Hermann Broch*, Rhein-Verlag, Zürich (Foto Sol Libsohn). 69 *Georg Trakl*, Otto Müller Verlag, Salzburg; *Rudolf Borchardt*, Ernst Klett Verlag, Stuttgart; *Theodor Däubler*, Kösel-Verlag, München (Foto Dr. Löffler, Dresden); *Walter Benjamin*, Suhrkamp Verlag, Frankfurt/Main. 70 *Else Lasker-Schüler*, Ullstein-Bilderdienst, Berlin. 71 *Karl Kraus*, Kösel-Verlag, München. 72 *Frank Wedekind*, Süddeutscher Verlag, München, Bild-Archiv; *Ferdinand Bruckner*, Akademie der Künste, Berlin-Dahlem, Ferdinand Bruckner-Archiv (Foto Dührkoop, Berlin); *Ernst Toller*, Schiller-Nationalmuseum, Marbach; *Georg Kaiser*, Akademie der Künste, Berlin-Dahlem, Georg Kaiser-Archiv. 73 *Heinrich Mann*, Aufbau-Verlag, Berlin. 74 *Oskar Loerke*, Suhrkamp Verlag, Frankfurt/Main. 75 *Gottfried Benn*, Limes Verlag, Wiesbaden (Foto Rama, Berlin). 76 *Erich Kästner*, Süddeutscher Verlag, München, Bild-Archiv. 101 *Stefan Andres*, R. Piper & Co Verlag, München; *Hermann Kasack*, Suhrkamp Verlag, Frankfurt/Main; *René Schickele*, Verlag Kiepenheuer & Witsch, Köln (Reproduction of drawing by Ludwig Kirchner); *Ernst Penzoldt*, Foto Herbert Römer, Braubach/Rhein. 102 *Luise Rinser*, S. Fischer Verlag, Frankfurt/Main (Foto Madeleine Winkler-Betzendahl, Stuttgart); *Elisabeth Langgässer*, Claassen Verlag, Hamburg; *Gertrud von Le Fort*, Franz Ehrenwirth-Verlag, München; *Ina Seidel*, Deutsche Verlags-Anstalt, Stuttgart (Foto Swiridoff, Schwäb. Hall). 103 *Ricarda Huch*, Insel-Verlag, Frankfurt/Main (Foto Willi Klar, Frankfurt/Main). 104 *Carl Zuckmayer*, S. Fischer Verlag, Frankfurt/Main (Foto Harald Meisert, Frankfurt/Main). 105 *Leonhard Frank*, Nymphenburger Verlagshandlung, München. 106 *Georg von der Vring*, Nymphenburger Verlagshandlung, München; *Karl Krolow*, Suhrkamp Verlag, Frankfurt/Main; *Georg Britting*, Nymphenburger Verlagshandlung, München; *Wilhelm Lehmann*, Süddeutscher Verlag, München, Bild-Archiv. 107 *Werner Bergengruen*, Nymphenburger Verlagshandlung, München. 108 *Hans Carossa*, in the possession of Professor Hans Wimmer, München (Foto Fellermeier). 133 *Heimito von Doderer*, Biederstein Verlag, München. 134 *Friedrich Dürrenmatt*, Verlag der Arche, Zürich. 135 *Max Frisch*, Suhrkamp Verlag, Frankfurt/Main. 136 *Rudolf Hagelstange*, R. Piper & Co Verlag, München (Foto Lauterwasser, Überlingen/Bodensee). 137 *Wolfgang Borchert*, Rowohlt Verlag, Reinbek (Foto Rosemarie Clausen, Hamburg). 138 *Heinrich Böll*, Verlag Kiepenheuer & Witsch, Köln (Foto Wack, Köln). 139 *Hans Erich Nossack*, Suhrkamp Verlag, Frankfurt/Main. 140 *Arno Schmidt*, Stahlberg Verlag, Karlsruhe (Foto Barth); *Wolfdietrich Schnurre*, Walter-Verlag, Freiburg und Olten; *Martin Walser*, Süddeutscher Verlag, München, Bild-Archiv; *Kurt Kusenberg*,

Rowohlt Verlag, Reinbek (Foto Gabriele, Hamburg). 141 *Günter Eich*, Suhrkamp Verlag, Frankfurt/Main (Foto Gaby Arnim, München). 142 *Ingeborg Bachmann*, R. Piper & Co Verlag, München. 143 *Marie Luise Kaschnitz*, Claassen Verlag, Hamburg (Foto Anny Breer, Hamburg). 144 *Alfred Andersch*, Walter-Verlag, Freiburg und Olten. 145 *Felix Hartlaub*, S. Fischer Verlag, Frankfurt/Main; *Gerd Gaiser*, Carl Hanser Verlag, München (Foto Theodora Layer); *Walter Jens*, R. Piper & Co Verlag, München; *Hans Magnus Enzensberger*, Suhrkamp Verlag, Frankfurt/Main. 146 *Günter Grass*, Hermann Luchterhand Verlag, Neuwied. 147 *Uwe Johnson*, Süddeutscher Verlag, München, Bild-Archiv. 148 *Wolfgang Koeppen*, Henry Goverts Verlag, Stuttgart (Foto Ruth Schramm, München).

Further illustrative material was kindly made available by: Präsident Dr. C. F. W. Behl, München. Dr. h. c. Werner Bergengruen, Baden-Baden. Biederstein Verlag, München. Georg Britting, München. Deutsche Verlags-Anstalt, Stuttgart. S. Fischer Verlag, Frankfurt/Main. Frau Charlotte Frank, München. Carl Hanser Verlag, München. Insel-Verlag, Frankfurt/Main. Verlag Kiepenheuer & Witsch, Köln. Kösel-Verlag, München. Alfred Kröner Verlag, Stuttgart. Verlag Helmut Küpper, vormals Georg Bondi, München. Albert Langen-Georg Müller Verlag, München. Hermann Luchterhand Verlag, Neuwied. Thomas Mann-Archiv, Zürich. Otto Müller Verlag, Salzburg. Frau Friedi Penzoldt, München. R. Piper & Co Verlag, München. Rowohlt Verlag, Reinbek. Schiller-Nationalmuseum, Marbach. Stahlberg Verlag, Karlsruhe. Suhrkamp Verlag, Frankfurt/Main.

Special reference is made to the following works which proved a valuable source of dieas in selecting the illustrative material:
Autoren der Gegenwart, Dichter; Gütersloh 1958; Begegnungen mit dem Buch in der Jugend, Reutlingen 1957; Deutsche Dichtung um 1900 / Handschriften, Bildnisse, Drucke / exhibition in the Schiller-Nationalmuseum, Marbach Mai - Oktober 1956; Stefan George in Selbstzeugnissen und Bilddokumenten, interpreted by Franz Schonauer, Rowohlt Monographie, Reinbek 1960; Expressionismus, Literatur und Kunst 1910-23, published by Bernhard Zeller, München 1960; Menschheitsdämmerung, Ein Dokument des Expressionismus, new edition by Kurt Pinthus, Reinbek 1959; Martin Möbius (Otto Julius Bierbaum), Steckbriefe, Berlin und Leipzig 1900; Alfred Richard Meyer, 1882-1956, Dichter, Schriftsteller, Verleger / Munkepunke / Bücher, Flugblätter, Autographen, Nürnberg Antiquariatskatalog 69; Ernst Penzoldt, Was der Welt ich abgeguckt, München 1956; Rilkes Leben und Werk im Bild, edited by Ingeborg Schnack, Wiesbaden 1956; Georg Kurt Schauer, Kleine Geschichte des deutschen Buchumschlags im 20. Jahrhundert, Königstein im Taunus 1962; Albert Soergel-Curt Hohoff, Dichter und Dichtung der Zeit, 2 Vols, Düsseldorf 1961-63; Welttheater, published by Siegfried Melchinger und Henning Rischbieter, Braunschweig 1962; Gero von Wilpert, Deutsche Literatur in Bildern, Stuttgart 1956.